"DOES THIS SHOCK YOU?"

Louis Kaczmarek

Published by:

M.B.S.

PO Box 1701, Plattsburgh, NY 12901
Phone (518) 561-8193 Fax (518) 566-7103
E-mail: ACFP2000@aol.com   Website: www.ACFP2000.com

DEDICATION

To all Christians to whom Our Lord spoke words of eternal life: "I am the living bread that came down from heaven; whoever eats this bread will live forever; and the bread that I will give is my flesh for the life of the world" (Jn 6:51), and lamented "there are some of you who do not believe" (Jn 6:64).

TABLE OF CONTENTS

Foreword

Some people are shocked to discover that Jesus is truly and personally present in the Holy Eucharist; He longs for us in the Blessed Sacrament day and night! Even more shocking may be the witness of the faithful throughout the ages whom Louis Kaczmarek describes as sacrificing not only their time—but in some cases their livelihood and very lives—to worship Jesus, hidden under the form of bread.

What impressed me most about this latest book by Louis is his tremendous love for the Sacred Eucharistic Heart of Jesus, and the body Jesus established to give us the Holy Mass and the Holy Eucharist: the Catholic Church. There are anecdotes and quotes from the saints which are very interesting and enjoyable to read. This was also illustrated in Louis' last book *The Eucharist and The Rosary: The Power to Change the World*, where he mentioned St. Elizabeth Ann Seton, the first canonized Saint of America. So great was her longing for the Presence of Jesus in the Holy Eucharist that, before she converted to Catholicism, St. Elizabeth gazed out the window of her Protestant Church— her eyes fixed on the nearby Catholic Church, where she knew Jesus dwelt in the tabernacle. It was her faith in the Real Presence which led to her conversion.

This is why throughout his life, beginning as a young man, Archbishop Fulton J. Sheen never missed his daily Holy Hour with Jesus in the Most Blessed Sacrament each morning. In the beginning of his autobiography *A Treasure in Clay*, Archbishop Sheen gave witness to the awesome movement of hundreds of thousands of Catholics and non-Catholics, who were inspired to accept his challenge of making a daily Holy Hour. Everyone that spends time in adoration of Jesus in the Blessed Sacrament develops a personal relationship with Him, and grows in love and holiness. Quiet time with the Lord teaches people to listen and recognize His voice as He speaks to their hearts. Many who attend adoration report miracles and healings. Communities experience increased Mass attendance, service of others, unity, conversions, and vocations to the priesthood and religious life.

Louis did not write his book to fill your mind with factual data. He would rather inflame your heart with an unquenchable love for Jesus and lead you to understand the greatest of all treasures is to be found only in the Catholic Church, Jesus Himself truly present in the Most Blessed Sacrament. If you are Catholic, reading this book will increase your love for the Church and the Bread of Eternal Life. If you are thinking about becoming Catholic, Louis' book will guide you on your journey to discover the greatest Love you will ever find on earth, the Real Presence of Jesus in the tabernacles of every Catholic Church in the world! Once you have made this discovery may you share it with others. Our Lady of the Most Blessed Sacrament and St. Joseph, Patron of the Universal Church, pray for us!

Fr. Lawrence Villone, M.S.L.B.S.

The Holy Eucharist is a direct and immediate encounter with Jesus Christ, God and man. Just as God said, "Let there be light," and there was light (Gen 1:3); through the medium of the priest, the bread and wine, in receiving the word of God, become the Word of God. Hence would St. Francis of Assisi say, "What wonderful majesty! What stupendous condescension! O sublime humility! That the Lord of the whole universe, God and the Son of God, should humble Himself like this under the form of a little bread, for our salvation."

Every person can truly say that an eternity is not sufficient to fathom God's infinite love for me – it requires heaven! From the Holy Eucharist alone can we gather His infinite goodness and love; the intimacy between God and man reaches its pinnacle; the embrace between God and man becomes total. Frequent reception of the Holy Eucharist brings me the most perfect union with Jesus that is possible in this earthly life.

The only place where you can receive the valid Holy Eucharist is the Catholic Church because of Apostolic succession – that direct-line connection from the original apostles to the present Catholic bishops. That's the critical juncture whereby valid bishops ordain valid priests who can celebrate valid Masses that can give us the Holy Eucharist.

"If your faith convinces you," said Fr. Isidore Mikulski, "that the Catholic Eucharist is absolutely, positively the real presence of Jesus Christ you will climb every mountain, cross every sea, even tolerate lousy liturgy to get to it."

I HAVE TASTED YOU AND AM HUNGRY FOR YOU

"I know men," said Napoleon, "and I tell you that Jesus Christ is not a man. Superficial minds see a resemblance between Christ and the founders of empires and the gods of other religions. That resemblance does not exist. There is between Christianity and whatever other religion the distance of infinity. Between Christ and whomsoever else in the world there is no possible term of comparison . . . . His birth, the history of His life, the profundity of His doctrine, His Gospel, His apparitions, His Empire, His march across the ages and realms – everything is for me a prodigy, a mystery insoluble . . . .

"Here I see nothing human . . . . His Revelation is a Revelation from an Intelligence which certainly is not that of man . . . . With what authority does He teach men to pray! . . . You speak of Caesar, of Alexander; of their conquests, and of the enthusiasm they kindled in the hearts of their soldiers; but can you conceive of a *dead* man making conquests with an army faithful and entirely devoted to his memory? My armies have forgotten me, even while living, as the Carthaginian army forgot Hannibal. Such is our power. A single battle lost crushes us, and adversity scatters our friends . . . . How different is the power of the God of the Christians, and the perpetual miracle of the progress of the faith and government of His Church! Nations pass away, thrones crumble, but the Church remains . . . . It is true, that Christ proposes to our faith a series of mysteries; but He commands with authority that we should believe them, giving no other reason than those tremendous words – I AM GOD!

"What an abyss He creates by that declaration between Himself and all the fabricators of religion! What audacity, what sacrilege, what blasphemy, if it were not true . . . Behold the approaching fate of him who has been called the great Napoleon! What an abyss between my profound misery and the eternal reign of Christ, which is proclaimed, loved and adored, and is extending over all the earth! Is this to die? Is it not rather to live? The death of Christ! It is the death of a God!"

When he was dying in exile on the island of St. Helena, May 5, 1821, Napoleon said: "The happiest day in my life was the day I made my first Holy Communion."

In early youth, St. Augustine fell into evil ways and until the age of thirty-two led a morally defiled life, wallowing in sin. After his conversion he wrote: "Plato gave me knowledge of the true God; Jesus Christ showed me the way . . . . I have tasted you and am hungry for you."

A FLASH OF LIGHTNING

The anti-Christian critic, Ernest Renan, said that in the first Century Christianity was like a flash of lightning which almost simultaneously lighted up the three peninsulas of Asia Minor, Greece and Italy.

After Christ's Resurrection, and the coming of the Holy Spirit on the Apostles—our first ordained priests—the Mass has been offered every day. It was not easy for Christians in Rome to risk their lives by having Mass in the underground catacombs. But they had Mass, as often as they could.

The 2,000-year-old history of the Catholic Church is the most historic and long-lasting of any organization on earth. Each century after the first, Christians knew their ancestors had attended Mass – to receive the Bread of Life – with the exception of converts to the Church, who then established the tradition for their descendants.

We are familiar with the persecution of Catholics under Communism, worse in some places than in others. We read of priests being imprisoned for decades in countries like in Communist China, just as they were in the Soviet Union, and as they are today in countries like Vietnam, Laos, Cambodia, North Korea and, to a considerable extent, in Cuba.

We are less familiar with the persecution Catholics suffered in countries like England, starting with Henry VIII. It was even worse in Ireland, where every Catholic Church was confiscated. To this day, both of the pre-Reformation cathedrals in Dublin are still in Protestant hands: St. Patrick's Cathedral and Christ Church.

During the more than 250 years of persecution of Catholics in Ireland, boys were often smuggled out of the country on fishing boats, to come back as priests years later. It was the great King Philip II of Spain who built three Irish seminaries for such youth: one in Spain, one in Paris, and one in Rome. Those seminaries were still operating until recently, though seminaries began to be tolerated by the English government in Ireland about 200 years ago, the first being Maynooth.

THE CHAPEL

Ireland remained more than 90 percent Catholic, and small chapels were finally permitted (few, if any, churches were ever given back). To ask for the Catholic Church in Ireland just 50 years ago, you asked for "the chapel." It had become a disgrace to say of someone: "He is going to church now." It meant he had given up his Catholic faith.

When Irish-born Archbishop Glennon of St. Louis, Missouri, was asked to speak at the International Eucharistic Congress in Dublin in 1933, he recalled how Ireland did not have stately cathedrals built over the centuries, because Catholicism had been so severely persecuted by England after Henry VIII broke from Rome. But Ireland had its hidden holy places such as "Mass rocks" he pointed out, where the Holy Sacrifice had been offered, in hiding from British police.

"Italy has its many Saints," Archbishop Glennon recalled, "and France has her stately cathedrals." Before he spoke of Ireland's practice of the Faith, despite persecution, he could not help but add: "and England has her regrets."

When a teenage boy in Seattle told his Irish-born father that the Episcopal cathedral had put in a statue of Mary, the dad smiled. When the boy told his dad a month later, "Now they are putting in the Fourteen Stations of the Cross," his father commented: "They are trying to get back what they lost." There was no way, however, they could put back the Mass and the Holy Eucharist. The priestly line of Apostolic succession had been irretrievably lost – and it is the real presence of God in the Blessed Sacrament that makes Catholicism a religion quite distinct from all Protestant denominations.

THE LOSS IN NORTHERN EUROPE

It was not only in England and Ireland that Catholics lost their churches. Half of Germany became Lutheran. Catholics were cut off from the church of their ancestors in so many places, including all of Sweden, Norway and Denmark, as well as in large parts of Holland. France, Italy, Spain and Portugal were the only countries where Europeans were allowed to practice their faith, except in Eastern European countries such as Poland, where they lost their churches later, under Communist conquest led by Russia.

Can you imagine how so many millions of Catholics suffered, losing their churches and above all, the opportunity to attend Mass and receive the Holy Eucharist! For Catholics to go to the church they had always attended, and hear nothing but some songs and a sermon was a terrible letdown. Under Communism, of course, it was even worse. Attending Mass often led to imprisonment or, at least, unemployment.

We are familiar with the hatred of Christianity under Communism. But how was it that the Reformation did away with the Mass? Isn't Christ's teaching about the consecration of bread and wine very clear? One explanation was made by Dr. Scott Hahn recently. Before he became a Catholic ten years ago, he taught in a Protestant seminary. When it came to an explanation of what Christ taught at the Last Supper, and His plea: "Do this in memory of me" (Lk 22:19-20), Hahn said he and his fellow professors skipped all that, turning the pages of Scripture to the next Gospel.

Obviously, they had no explanation for not having the Mass and the Holy Eucharist, except that they were not validly ordained as priests. But how shocked the millions of Catholics were to find, all of a sudden, that Mass was no longer celebrated in their church and the Holy Eucharist was not available.

HOLY MASS IS THE SACRIFICE OF THE CROSS

Vatican Council II teaches, "At the Last Supper, the night in which He was betrayed, Jesus initiated the Eucharistic Sacrifice of His Body and Blood, in order to continue the Sacrifice of the Cross throughout the centuries until His return" (The Constitution on the Liturgy, 47).

St. Leonard of Port Maurice said, "I believe that if there were no Mass, the world would by now have sunk into the abyss under the weight of its wickedness. The Mass is the powerful support which sustains it."

"The celebration of the Holy Mass," wrote St. Thomas Aquinas, "is as valuable as the death of Jesus on the Cross." And St. Alphonsus Liguori said, "God Himself cannot bring about an action more holy and greater than the celebration of one Holy Mass."

When St. Padre Pio of Pietrelcina was asked, "Father, please explain the Holy Mass to us," he replied, "My children, how can I explain it to you? The Mass is infinite like Jesus . . . . ask an Angel what a Mass is and he will reply to you in truth, 'I understand what it is and why it is offered, but I do not, however, understand how much value it has.' One Angel, a thousand Angels, all of Heaven, know this and think like this."

We can almost take for granted that angels appear at the Altar at the Consecration of the Mass. Their presence is best described as "the unheard fluttering of unseen wings." We can only see them with our mind's eye, our soul.

Just as an angel is with each of us as long as we are on earth, why wouldn't a myriad of angels be there to honor Our Lord when He is actually and physically present on the Altar? Where else is the Holy Sacrifice of Calvary renewed so wonderfully? In no other way can we honor Jesus so much, than by kneeling there at the Altar as He asked: "Do this in remembrance of Me."

Jesus doesn't need us there. But He loves us with an infinite love and He knows, far more than we, how greatly we need Him. Nothing more than our attendance at Mass can prepare us so well for an eternity with Jesus. In no other way does He strengthen us so spiritually.

THE HOLY SACRIFICE OF THE MASS IS SCRIPTURAL

Melchizedeck, the King of Salem, was a priest who offered sacrifice under the form of bread and wine (Gen 4:18). Psalm 109 predicts that Christ will be a priest according to the order of Melchizedeck, that is, offering sacrifice under the forms of bread and wine.

The Prophet Malachi predicts a new sacrifice to be offered in every place. "From the rising of the sun even to the going down my name is great among the Gentiles: and in every place there is sacrifice and there is offered to my name a clean oblation" (Mal 1:11).

Referring to Malachi's prophecy, Fr. Carty said, "The Sacrifice of Calvary took place in one place only. We must look for a sacrifice apart from Calvary, one offered in every place under the forms of bread and wine. The Mass is that Sacrifice."

Saint Thomas Aquinas called the Mass "the holy banquet in which Christ is received, the memory of His Passion is recalled, the soul is filled with grace, and there is given to us a pledge of future glory."

Because the Holy Sacrifice of the Mass is the work of God whereby His Body and Blood are offered to man, all the good works that man has performed – in the history of the world – cannot equal the value of one Holy Mass! "After the Consecration," said St. John Vianney, "the good God is there as He is in Heaven. If man well understood this mystery, he would die of love."

We should be on fire with zeal to attend Mass daily! Continuously through twenty centuries, the Sacrifice of the Mass has been offered in the Catholic Church, and is today offered in every place from the rising of the sun even to its going down, as Malachi predicted!

DAILY MASS

Breastplate against the world's despising thrusts;
Buckler to face foul sin's distracting gusts!
Sword in the hand to make protecting pass - The Daily Mass!

Staff to support when climbing Life's steep hill -
Robe to enwrap when adverse winds   blow chill.
Soon to make stoniest roads as softest grass – The Daily Mass!

Shelter against all foes' unkindly sneers;
Courage to meet and scorn Death's threatening fears!
Greatest of Acts to help drear days to pass –
The Daily Mass!

Food to revive the thirsting soul and frail –
Drink to restore, lest flesh and spirit fail!
Sweetness Divine, in this Rite all woes pass –
The Daily Mass!

CHAPTER TWO—NOTHING IS MORE PLEASING TO GOD

"A soul can do nothing that is more pleasing to God," said St. Alphonsus Liguori, "than to communicate in a state of grace." What indispensable joy is ours when Jesus Himself becomes our guest! He does not become part of us; we become part of Him! St. Hilary said "Having received the Body and Blood of Christ, we are in Christ and Christ is in us."

Is there anything that can excite a soul more than to realize that the Eucharist unites us to Christ directly? It is the Sacrament of union referred to as Holy Communion and which Webster's dictionary translates as "possession in communion" because we are literally penetrated by Jesus, plunged into the divinity the very moment the Sacred Host enters our bodies! It is a union of Christ and our soul that could not possibly be more intimate – His blood flows through our veins; his flesh is enmeshed with our flesh; his soul unites with our soul, and we are immersed in the Divinity! Christ physically becomes a part of every cell in our body through the valid reception of the Holy Eucharist!

"No union between the Creator and the creature," said Fr. Frederick Faber, "has been devised so awfully intimate as the Sacramental Union; neither has the creature in any other mystery been lifted to such a height as that he should be allowed, with a reality so real that no word is forcible enough to express it, to make his Creator his daily Bread."

St. Ignatius speaks of this tremendous intimacy in his prayer to be said after receiving Holy Communion: "Soul of Christ, sanctify me. Body of Christ, save me. Blood of Christ, inebriate me. Water from the side of Christ, wash me. Passion of Christ, strengthen me. O good Jesus, hear me. Within Thy wounds, hide me. Suffer me not to be separated from Thee. From the malicious enemy, defend me. In the hour of my death, call me. And bid me come to Thee. That with Thy saints, I may praise Thee. For ever and ever. Amen."

In document nine, issued by the Sacred Congregation of Rites in the Second Vatican Council, it states, "For 'the partaking of the Body and Blood of Christ has no less an effect than to change us into what we have received.'"

Only saints can truly appreciate this total union with Jesus in the Holy Eucharist:

1) St. Francis de Sales: "Nowhere do we find Our Savior more tender or more loving than here where He, so to speak, annihilates Himself and reduces Himself to food in order to penetrate our souls and to unite Himself to the hearts of His friends."

2) Pope John Paul II: "The Holy Eucharist contains the entire spiritual treasure of the Church, that is, Christ Himself, our Passover and living bread."

3) St. Peter Julian Eymard: "The Eucharist is the supreme proof of the love of Jesus. After this, there is nothing more but heaven . . . . Be willing to sacrifice everything, be willing to do everything for the sake of one communion. A single communion is able to transform a sinner into a saint instantaneously, because it is Jesus Christ Himself, author of all sanctity, who comes to you."

4) St. Gemma Galgani: "It is not possible to have a union of love more profound and more total: He in me and I in Him; the one in the other. What more could we want?"

5) St. John Vianney: "Of all the Sacraments, there is not one that can be compared to the Holy Eucharist . . . a soul may receive its Creator, and as often as it desires."

6) St. John Chrysostom: "How many in these times say: would that I could gaze upon His form, His figure; His garment, His shoes! Thou seest Him, thou touchest Him, eatest Him. He gives Himself to thee, not merely to look upon, but even to touch, to eat, and to receive within . . . . Consider at Whose table thou eatest! For we are fed with that which the angels view with trepidation and which they cannot contemplate without fear because of its splendor. We become one with Him; we become one body and one flesh with Christ."

THE GRADUATE SCHOOL OF DIVINE LOVE

Archbishop Fulton J. Sheen said that Adoration of Jesus in the Most Blessed Sacrament is radioactive. As you sit before the Sacred Host in Adoration, the Host eats away faults and sins in the soul that cannot be overcome by either prayer or penance.

The noted English writer, J. R. R. Tolkien, loved his Catholic Faith. The heart and soul of his love was the Holy Eucharist, and Christ's presence in the Mass. To him this was the graduate school of divine love. When his son, Michael, said that his faith was weakening, Tolkien wrote to him:

"The only cure for sagging Faith is Communion. The Blessed Sacrament does not operate completely and once for all, in any of us. Like an act of faith it must be continuous, and grow by exercise. Frequency is of the highest effect.

"The chief claim of the Church is that it has always defended the Blessed Sacrament, given it most honor, and put it, as Christ plainly intended, in the prime place."

Tolkien later wrote Michael: "I set before you the one great thing to love on earth: the Blessed Sacrament. There you will find romance, honor, fidelity, and the true way of all your loves on earth."

What is unique about Tolkien's approach to his religion, and his advice pertaining to it, is that he was always practical with emphasis on action and deeds. And the dominant thought running through all his writing on this subject is his devotion to the Blessed Sacrament. In one of his letters he wrote: "It takes a fantastic will of unbelief to suppose that Jesus never really 'happened', and more to suppose that he did not say the things recorded of him – so incapable of being 'invented' by anyone in the world at that time: such as 'before Abraham came to be I am' (Jn 8); 'He that hath seen me hath seen the Father' (Jn 9); or the promulgation of the Blessed Sacrament in John 6: 'He that eats my flesh and drinks my blood has eternal life.'"

Tolkien was convinced that Our Lord's words "Feed my sheep" referred primarily to the "Bread of Life," the Holy Eucharist. And where can we find continuity more marvelous than the Real Presence of our Lord in the Holy Eucharist who is with us all days even until the end of the world! How many of us would simplify our spiritual lives if we would only look to the Blessed Sacrament, to our conduct towards it and its impression upon us, as the index of our spiritual progress.

We always try to awaken ourselves with new ideas, new books, new prayers, and new states of prayer. How much better it would be to focus our attention on the presence of Jesus in the Blessed Sacrament who will be the judge upon whom our entrance into eternal life depends.

THE GREAT PRESENCE

In his novel, *Loss or Gain,* Ven. John Henry Newman describes the hero of the novel entering a Catholic Church for the first time. It is not the beauty of the liturgy that impresses him, as much as it is "the Great Presence, which makes a Catholic Church different from every other place in the world."

Here is how the scholarly Newman confirms his complete faith in the Holy Eucharist, and explains why his faith is so certain:

"I betake myself to one of our altars to receive the Blessed Eucharist. I have no doubt whatever in my mind about the Gift which that Sacrament contains. I confess to myself my belief, and I go through the steps on which it is assured to me.

"The Presence of Christ is here, for it follows upon Consecration; and Consecration is the prerogative of Priests; and Priests are made by Ordination; and Ordination comes in direct line from the Apostles.

"Whatever be our other misfortunes, every link in our chain is safe. We have the Apostolic Succession. We have a right form of Consecration. Therefore we are blessed with the great Gift."

"Here the question rises in me: 'Who told you about that Gift?' I answer, "I have learned it from the great Fathers and Doctors of the Church. I believe the Real Presence because they were witness to it."

Newman summed it all up when he wrote: "There is no benedictionfrom earth of sky which falls upon us like that which comes to us from the Blessed Sacrament, which is Himself."

NOTHING THIS SIDE OF HEAVEN EQUALS THE HOLY EUCHARIST

The real cause of the Church's spiritual triumph is because she has Jesus Himself with her, the Living God, in the Blessed Sacrament. It is this real presence of God which makes Catholicism a religion quite distinct from all Protestant faiths. Interestingly enough, it is the Sacrament that Jesus Himself received; it is the greatest work of God! Next to the Beatific Vision, it is the surest, the happiest, and the nearest sight of God that we can enjoy.

In no place in Sacred Scripture does it show any disagreement on the doctrine of the Holy Eucharist. And if there is one dignity of the Holy Eucharist which is more undeniable than another, it is that it is the queen of the Sacraments, the fountain of immortal grace! No others can compare with it; for while the others bring us the precious gifts of Jesus, the Holy Eucharist brings us what is unspeakably more precious, Jesus, God and Man, Himself!

"The love of the Blessed Sacrament," said Fr. Frederick Faber, "is the grand and royal devotion of faith; it is faith multiplied, faith intensified, faith glorified, and yet remaining faith still, while it is glory also. And out of it there comes three special graces which are the very life and soul of an interior life: an overflowing charity to all around us, a thirst to sacrifice ourselves for God, and a generous and filial love of Holy Church."

Nothing this side of Heaven can equal the Body of Christ in the Holy Eucharist! Jesus always sends rays of light to everyone who nourishes their love for Him in adoration before the Blessed Sacrament. And when you receive Him in Holy Communion you receive not only the Author of life, but the Author of sanctity. Fr. John T. Myler said it beautifully:

"Think of the greatest banquet ever thrown: the Body of Christ is greater!
Think of the most exquisite fruits on a tropical table: the Body of Christ is greater!
Think of the choicest meats, the finest drink: the Body of Christ is greater!
Think of the most powerful of human nourishments: The Body of Christ is greater!
Think of the most energizing of all food and fare: the Body of Christ is greater!
Think of the most sublime of testimonials: the Body of Christ is greater!
Think of the most revered of human rituals: the Body of Christ is greater!
Think of the most sociable of settings: the Body of Christ is greater!

Think of the most costly of banquets: the Body of Christ is greater!
Think of one man's grandest tribute to another: the Body of Christ is greater!
Think of all history's gallant efforts to give glory: the Body of Christ is greater!"

ST. PAUL, COUNCIL OF TRENT, AN ANGEL

In the 1st century St. Paul said: "Therefore whoever eats the bread or drinks the cup of the Lord unworthily will have to answer for the body and blood of the Lord" (1 Cor 11:27).

In the 16th century, the Council of Trent stated: "If anyone shall deny that the Sacrament of the Blessed Eucharist contains truly, really and substantially the body and blood, together with the soul and divinity of Our Lord Jesus Christ, and consequently Christ whole and entire . . . let him be anathema [damned]."

In the 20th century an Angel appeared to the three children of Fatima holding a golden chalice in his left hand. Above the chalice in his right hand he held a Consecrated Host. Drops of Blood were falling from the Host into the chalice. Leaving both suspended in the air, prostrating himself upon the ground, the angel taught the three children to pray this prayer which he prayed three times: "O Most Holy Trinity – Father, Son, and Holy Spirit – I adore Thee profoundly. I offer Thee the most precious Body, Blood, Soul and Divinity of Jesus Christ, present in all the tabernacles of the world, in reparation for the outrages, sacrileges and indifferences by which He is offended. Through the infinite merits of the Sacred Heart of Jesus and the Immaculate Heart of Mary, I beg you for the conversion of poor sinners."

INDISPUTABLE DOCTRINE OF THE EUCHARIST

Pope Paul VI in his 1965 encyclical on the Eucharist, *Mysterium Fidei* (the Mystery of Faith), declared that "one cannot be a Catholic if one does not accept the teaching of the Council of Trent on the Eucharist in its entirety."

The doctrine of the real presence of Jesus Christ in the Eucharist is the easiest doctrine to prove from Sacred Scripture and it is also the most attractive and compelling – and the biggest reason why converts join the Catholic Church!

Of this truth, and all that Christ taught, the Apostles were so convinced that they gave their lives!

St. Peter was crucified upside down.
St. Andrew was bound to a cross in the shape of an "X."
St. James, the son of Zebedee, was put to death by the Jews.
St. Thomas was martyred in India.
St. James, son of Alphaeus, was stoned to death.

St. Philip suffered and died on a cross.

St. Bartholomew was, according to tradition, flayed alive.

St. Matthew was martyred.

Sts. Simon and Jude Thaddeus were martyred together.

St. Matthias was, according to the Greeks, crucified in Colcis.

St. John was the only Apostle to die a natural death. He suffered many attempts on his life before dying of old age. He remained to confirm that Christ is literally present in the Holy Eucharist and not symbolically as Protestants claim. Count the times in the sixth chapter, verses 48-58, in St. John's Gospel, called "the Gospel of love," that Christ emphatically repeats the literal teaching of this truth – line after shocking line:

(verse 48): "I am the bread of life."

(verse 49): "Your ancestors ate the manna in the desert, but they died; this is the bread that comes down from heaven so that one may eat it and not die."

(verse 51): "I am the living bread that came down from heaven; whoever eats this bread will live forever; and the bread I will give is my flesh for the life of the world."

(verse 53): "Amen, amen, I say to you, unless you eat the flesh of the Son of Man and drink his blood, you do not have life within you."

(verse 54): "Whoever eats my flesh and drinks my blood has eternal life, and I will raise him up on the last day."

(verse 55): "My flesh is real food and my blood is real drink."

(verse 56): "Whoever eats my flesh and drinks my blood remains in me and I in him."

(verse 57): "Just as the living father sent me and I have life because of the Father, so also the one who feeds on me will have life because of me."

(verse 58): "This is the bread that came down from heaven. Unlike your ancestors who ate and still died, whoever eats this bread will live forever."

(verse 61): **"Does this shock you?"**

No words Our Lord spoke were ever more relevant than **"Does this shock you?"** "See the esteem," said St. John Vianney, "in which Our Lord holds the Word of God! To the woman who cries, 'Blessed is the womb that bore Thee, and the breasts that gave Thee suck,' He answers, 'Yea, rather blessed are they who hear the Word of God and keep it!' Our Lord, Who is Truth itself, puts no less value on His Word than on His Body."

The more they refused to believe ("The Jews therefore murmured about him because he said, 'I am the bread that has come down from heaven'"; "This is a hard saying"; "Who can listen to it?"; "How can this man give us His flesh to eat?"), the more He insisted! "As a result of this, many of his disciples returned to their former way of life and no longer accompanied him" (Jn 6:66) – some of the saddest words in Sacred Scripture.

Does anyone actually believe that Jesus, God and Man, would let all of those disciples leave him if He did not truly mean what He said? If Jesus did not mean precisely what He said then why would He be willing to let the Apostles go too rather than retract His words: "Do you also want to leave?" (Jn 6:67). Simon Peter answered him, "Master, to whom shall we go? You have the words of eternal life. We have come to believe and are convinced that you are the Holy One of God" (Jn 6: 68-69).

Would He who said: "I am the way, and the truth, and the life" (Jn 14:6); "I came into the world, to testify to the truth" (Jn 8:58); "If I speak the truth, why do you not believe me?" (Jn 8:46) – deliberately deceive and confuse on such an essential teaching? A Hindu proverb says: "The name of God is truth!" It is ironic that Protestant fundamentalists accept everything the Bible says as literally true except Christ changing bread and wine into His body and blood.

In *The Question Box,* July 27-August 2, 2002 issue of *The Catholic Times,* Lansing Diocese of Michigan, Fr. Isidore J. Mikulski was presented with this question:

"It seems to me that Catholic belief in the Eucharist being the real, not symbolic, presence of Jesus is making trouble for us. It comes up every time non-Catholic relatives accompany us to Mass. They like to come but they can't go up for Communion with us. They say that's OK with them. How did we ever get ourselves in that position?"

Answer: "For such an impasse we must give credit to our earliest ancestors. They were unanimous in their belief that our Eucharist is absolutely, positively, really and truly the genuine presence of Jesus Christ, body, blood, soul and divinity.

"Besides the testimony of the Gospels and St. Paul's correspondence, the first generation of writer-theologians agreed on the real, not the symbolic, presence of Jesus Christ in the Eucharist. Ignatius, Justin, Irenaeus, Origin, Athanasius, Cyril – all those and others who were closest to the scene emphasized this indisputable doctrine of the Eucharist.

"St. Paul, with his customary bluntness, devotes half of chapter 11 in his first letter to the people in Corinth to the defense of this sacrament. He said 'anyone who eats and drinks without recognizing the body is eating and drinking his own condemnation.' He wouldn't have been so insistent if the Eucharist was just a nice, pious symbol.

"Justin, (d. 135 AD) writing the first-ever instruction book for converts, said 'This food we call Eucharist and no one may share it unless he believes our teaching is true . . . for we do not receive these things as though they were ordinary food and drink . . . it becomes the flesh and blood of the incarnate Jesus.'

"After 20 centuries of fidelity how could we possibly dilute that doctrine into just another nice, pious, symbol?"

THE FOUR EVANGELISTS

The Four Evangelists quote Christ's Divine authority on this matter and they not only affirm what he said, they actually equate his body and blood in the Eucharist with his body and blood offered on the cross! They, therefore, are both literally true or they are both symbolic!

(Mk 14:24): "This is my blood of the covenant, which will be shed for many."

(Lk 22:19): "This is my body, which will be given for you."

(Mt 26:28): "This is my blood of the covenant, which will be shed on behalf of many for the forgiveness of sins."

(Jn 6:51): "I am the living bread that came down from heaven; whoever eats this bread will live forever; and the bread that I will give is my flesh for the life of the world."

History proves Christ did offer his real flesh and blood on the cross – therefore His real flesh and blood are available to us in Holy Communion!

FAITH AND REASON

"The consecrated Host," said Fathers Rumble and Carty, "looks like bread, it tastes like bread, it nourishes like bread. There is no difference for a priest and layman. At the altar the priest has no experience at all of a change. Yet, after consecration, there is no substance of bread remaining. The Body, Blood, Soul and Divinity of Christ are present. Human reason tells us three things:

1) The God who created the universe with a mere act of His will is infinitely powerful, and not to be limited by the degrees of a created finite intelligence.

2) God is Truth Itself, and could not possibly tell us a lie.

3) The Gospels are true history. No documents have had such a thorough sifting. They have survived a deeper critical study, a more searching analysis than any other writings have had to undergo, and that not only by men of good will, but by the very enemies of Christianity.

"These three things are clear to our human reason. Unless a man receives additional light from God he will be unable to proceed, to grasp the full significance of the truths contained in the Gospels. That additional light is given by the Church that gave the Bible to the world. As reason told us three things, reason and Faith combined also tell us three things:

1) The historical Person described in the Gospel, and known as Jesus Christ, is Almighty God, with all divine attributes.

2) This Christ taught the doctrine of the Blessed Sacrament as clearly as it is possible to state it.

3) He also established an infallible Church, which guarantees to maintain the judgment of reason and Faith in accordance with God's knowledge of this matter.

We, therefore, believe with absolute certainty that Christ is really present in the Sacred Host."

The council of Trent in 1551 declared that "in the sacrament of the most Holy Eucharist is contained truly, really, and substantially the body and blood, together with the soul and divinity, of our Lord Jesus Christ, and consequently the whole Christ" (Denzinger 1636, 1640).

Fr. John A. Hardon, S.J., in his *Modern Catholic Dictionary*, page 457, says: "Hence Christ is present truly or actually and not only symbolically. He is present really, that is objectively in the Eucharist and not only subjectively in the mind of the believer. And he is present substantially, that is with all that makes Christ Christ and not only spiritually in imparting blessings on those who receive the sacrament. The one who is present is the whole Christ (*totus Christus*), with all the attributes of his divinity and all the physical parts and properties of his humanity."

Either the Eucharist is or it isn't the real presence of Jesus Christ! The comment of Catholic author Flannery O'Connor says it all. After listening to a group of ladies discuss how nice it seems to have the symbolic Jesus in their worship service she blurted out "If it isn't the body of Jesus Christ to hell with it."

25

CHAPTER THREE—WITHOUT THE MASS
IT IS NOT THE CHURCH CHRIST FOUNDED

The Book of Jesus, edited by Dr. Calvin Miller, a Baptist theology professor, is heralded as "a treasure of the greatest stories and writings about Christ." In some ways it is, but in the very essence of Christ's teachings, it is woefully lacking.

The 574-page book contains writings from 400 authors, from Billy Graham to Mother Teresa. Yet only once in this huge book is "blessing the bread and wine" mentioned, and that is only in passing, written by a non-Catholic.

No believer in the Mass is permitted to say anything about it. Nor is the Mass or the Holy Eucharist ever mentioned. The quotes of many Catholic theologians are merely a camouflage.

No book brings out so clearly the complete difference between the Catholic Church and all other Christian churches. No matter how well Christ's other teachings are mentioned, without the Mass and the Holy Eucharist it is not the Church Christ founded.

Any church service that consists of just sermons, songs, and Old or New Testament readings helter-skelter is void of reality when it excludes any mention of the consecration of bread and wine by an ordained priest.

The real church service is doing what Christ commanded us to do: to consecrate bread and wine and distribute it in Holy Communion "in remembrance of me." Nothing else is so directly connected to our redemption on the Cross.

The Mass is the highest ceremonial of the Church on earth, and the crown of all her ritual and worship is the exposition of the Blessed Sacrament. There is no better way to participate in His love so effectively and so beautifully, and to return our love to Him. The Mass is the renewal of Calvary!

Fr. Roger Amsparger, a former Baptist who converted to Catholicism, said "Catholicism, Christianity, does not exist without the Real Presence . . . . Christ wills to cooperate physically here and now in the production of the supernatural effects of the sacrifice of the cross. Christ as man wills each act of transubstantiation in virtue of an act of His will made while on earth, when He foresaw and willed every single Mass as an application of the merits of Calvary. This interior offering continues unceasingly in Christ – it is never renewed or multiplied."

The Mass is the self-same Sacrifice as was offered at the Last Supper and on Calvary! The Holy Sacrifice of the Mass is ever being said at an average of seven Consecrations a second is some part of the world, and each of these Masses gives infinite Glory and Joy and Love to God, to make up to Him for man's forgetfulness of heart; infinite reparation to God to make up for man's wickedness; infinite thanks to God to make up for man's ingratitude; infinite pleadings to God to make up for a world that has almost forgotten God. In his book *A Shepherd Speaks,* Bishop Fabian Bruskewitz wrote:

"A saint once said that, if you prayed and did penance every moment of your life and added to that all the prayers and merits of the Blessed Virgin Mary and the angels and saints, all of this would not even begin to equal the value of one Mass. For each Mass makes present again the dying and rising of Jesus Himself and the perfect adoration and gratitude He gives to God the Father through His paschal mystery . . . .

"A very old prayer calls the Mass an *admirable commercium,* or a 'marvelous exchange.' This is basically what the Mass is. Each part of the Mass is an exchange with God.

"In the first part of the Mass we exchange 'words' with God. We speak to Him, through Christ, in the Holy Spirit, in the prayer that the priest says on our behalf. We beg His forgiveness and praise His glory. Then, God speaks to us in the words of Holy Scripture, especially in the very words of Jesus in the Gospel, and in the preaching of the Church.

"In the second and more important part of the Mass, we exchange gifts with God. We give to God our bread and wine, which symbolize our work and recreation, our tears and smiles, our lives and ourselves. Our contribution in the collection basket also represents the gifts or ourselves . . . .

"Then, at the climax of the Mass, Christ takes our worthless gifts and changes them, through the invocation and blessing of the Holy Spirit and the words of institution, spoken by the ordained priest, into His gift of Himself to God. Thus, our gifts, joined to His, become of infinite worth and of unsurpassable value. This is what makes each Mass, even when imperfect with defective music, ceremonies, rubrics, or homily, infinitely meritorious before God.

"Finally, the exchange of gifts concludes when we receive back our gifts, now transformed and 'transubstantiated' into the Body and Blood of our Redeemer, in Holy Communion."

THE SANCTITY OF THE MASS

The Mass is of infinite value but the fruits are applied to us in a limited manner according to our faith and devotion, our disposition. The Mass brings us more grace, more of the Holy Spirit than anything else we can do. As Vatican II put it: "from the Eucharist, grace is poured forth upon us as from a fountain, and the sanctification of men in Christ and the glorification of God to which all other activities of the Church are directed, as toward their end, are achieved with maximum effectiveness." Nothing prepares us more for the divine nuptials than the Mass. When we go to Mass and participate with sincere effort and love, we also reduce our purgatorial debt tremendously.

28

In the Eucharist we offer the body Christ gave for us on the Cross, the very blood He poured out "for the forgiveness of sins." This is the visible sacrifice our mortal nature requires. As the Council of Trent declared, "The bloody sacrifice of the Cross is re-presented, perpetuated to the end of the world. Its salutary power is applied daily to the forgiveness of sins we daily commit."

The sacrifice of Christ and the sacrifice of the Mass are united, as one unique sacrifice. Only the manner of the offering is different. Quoting from the great Council of Trent: "In this divine sacrifice of the Mass, the same Christ who offered Himself once in a bloody manner now is offered in an unbloody manner." Yes, the wine is His body and blood, but it remains in the form of wine.

Our Lord's earthly ministry is over, and He now distributes the fruits of His Sacrifice from the Altar at Mass. At Mass we co-operate with Him in this distribution, and become carriers of His Redeeming Grace to the whole world.

Beautifully and marvelously, in the Mass the lives of the faithful – our praise, sufferings, prayers and works are united with Christ and with His total, infinite offering. Our offerings, small as they are in themselves, acquire great value, for we are united with His offering. Mass is offered in the name of the whole Church. It is like being at the foot of the Cross with Mary, united in the intercession of Christ.

Such is the sacrifice of Christians. St. Augustine wrote 1600 years ago: "We who are many are one Body in Christ." Christ is present in many ways in the Church, "where two or three are gathered together in my name," in the poor, the sick and the imprisoned.

How His love went out especially to those in prison! No mention of whether they are innocent or guilty, no more than the shepherd searching for the little lost lamb.

And what of the rejoicing in Heaven over one sinner who repents, even more than for 99 who need not repent! We are united in the Holy Sacrifice of the Mass. What a pity that a hundred million Christians were deprived of the Mass, and still are, by the Reformers. The great Council of Trent met for six years, shortly after, to try and clarify and defend the Mass. But little heed was taken by those who had left the Church, despite its authenticity prior to the Reformation, its saints and scholars, and 1600 years of long tradition.

Our Divine Lord's Real Presence in the Blessed Sacrament makes the Catholic Church not merely an impersonal creed, but a living, palpitating personal life that throbs with the Divine strength that infuses it. The "Living Bread come down from heaven" is drawn from every Catholic Altar, the living Blood flows in the life-giving streams from every Altar of Sacrifice.

29

This is the miracle of the Catholic Church, Emmanuel, God-with-us, not the multiplication of the loaves, but the multiplication of the Tabernacles. This glorious Presence is the center of all. It makes each Church, each Monastery, each convent a Heaven upon earth to which His tired children can come and be strengthened and be sustained by the Living Bread of God. This is the reason of His Presence in the Tabernacle.

"If anyone wishes to know how the bread is changed into the Body of Jesus Christ," said St. John Damascene, "I will tell him. The Holy Spirit overshadows the priest and acts on him as He acted on the Blessed Virgin Mary." Cardinal Manning of England once remarked that a priest saying "This is My Body" is using a sentence that has no equal except when God said: "Let there be light."

Here are the saving effects which every Holy Sacrifice of the Mass produces in the soul: It lessens the temporal punishment due to sins; It obtains pardon and sorrow for our sins; it strengthens the bonds of our union in the Body of Christ; it protects us from danger and disaster; it obtains a higher degree of glory in Heaven; it shortens the punishment of Purgatory; and it weakens the influence of Satan along with the untamed impulses of our flesh.

St. Thomas, the Prince of Theologians, said "The Mass obtains for sinners in mortal sin the grace of repentance. For the just, it obtains the remission of venial sins and the pardon of the pain due to sin. It obtains an increase of habitual [Sanctifying] grace, as well as all the graces necessary for their special needs."

St. Laurence Justinian concurs: "No human tongue can enumerate the favors that trace back to the Sacrifice of the Mass. The sinner is reconciled with God; the just man becomes more upright; sins are wiped away; vices eliminated; virtue and merit gain growth and the devil's schemes are frustrated."

THE PRECIOUS PRIVILEGE OF THE HOLY MASS

In his book *Calvary and the Mass: a Missal Companion*, Archbishop Fulton J. Sheen said: "Picture then the High Priest Christ leaving the sacristy of heaven for the altar of Calvary. He has already put on the vestment of our human nature, the maniple of our suffering, the stole of priesthood, the chasuble of the Cross. Calvary is His cathedral; the rock of Calvary is the altar stone; the sun turning to red is the sanctuary lamp; Mary and John are the living side altars; the host is His Body; the wine is His Blood. He is upright as Priest, yet He is prostrate as Victim. His Mass is about to begin."

Few have praised the Mass like John L. Stoddard, a famous English writer, who was raised a Calvinist, and entered a seminary with plans to be a missionary. There, however, the "intellectual chaos" of Protestantism turned him against Christianity, which he fought for the next 40 years – until World War I shocked him into a renewed spiritual quest that brought him all the way to the Catholic Church.

Though published in 1921, Stoddard's book *Rebuilding a Lost Faith,* reads as though it was written for our present crisis with such useful insights taking on Protestants and religious skeptics by providing ammunition against both Protestantism and atheism. Stoddard wrote "I was moved to write these pages by a desire to counteract the evil influence which my hostility to Christianity once exerted; and to undo the harm produced."

It was the Mass that impressed him and his wife more than anything. He describes his great appreciation of the Mass in his book. Here are highlights from his book:

"Of the many compensations that await the convert, the greatest, surely, is the precious privilege of the Holy Mass. It is the very soul of Catholicism, and the essence of Christianity.

"Slowly but irresistibly its beauty, mysticism and solemnity drew me to the Blessed Sacrament and to the Church that shelters it. The steps by which my faltering feet ascended to its altar were its ancient prayers. These, in connection with the ceremony itself, filled me with awe and admiration.

"Once a person realizes that Jesus was the Son of God, sent to redeem mankind from sin and punishment by His atoning sacrifice, the Mass becomes at once the greatest spiritual privilege, and the highest act of human adoration.

"It is the re-enactment of the sacrifices of Christ, the celebration of His death upon an altar, typifying Calvary. These, to the repentant worshipper, bring sanctifying grace.

"What overwhelmed me as a non-Catholic was the universality of the Mass. It thrills one, as he kneels before the elevated Host, to recollect that there is not a country—scarcely a city or hamlet in the civilized world—where this same ritual of the Mass is not said daily, often many times a day. Not an island rises from the sea, if it be tenanted by man, from which the supplication of the Mass does not ascend to God each day, like incense from an altar.

"Other religions are local. This is universal. Like an unbroken chain, it clasps the rounded globe, and holds it fast to God. Its service never ends. Its continuity sweeps round our planet, like the moving tides.

THE SUN NEVER SETS ON THE MASS
"At every moment, somewhere, as the earth revolves, the rising sun is shining on the symbol of Christ's sacrifice, upheld by the adoring celebrant, and on this Holy Eucharist that sun can never set.

31

"Somewhere before a Catholic altar the words are always being uttered: 'Lamb of God, who takes away the sins of the world, have mercy on us.' Yes, these identical words are used in every land, dear to the Saints and Martyrs of remote antiquity, and hallowed since by generations of the faithful—an example of the Church's universality and unity.

"When I am asked what I have found within the Catholic Church superior to all that Protestantism gave me, I find that language is inadequate to express it. One thinks of a stained-glass window in a vast cathedral.

"Seen from without by day, this seems to be an unintelligible mass of dusky glass. Viewed from within, however, it reveals a beautiful design, where sacred story glows in form and color.

"So it is with the Church of Rome. One must enter it to understand its sanctity and charm. When I reflect upon that Church's long, unbroken continuity extending back to the very days of the Apostles; when I recall her grand, inspiring traditions, her blessed Sacraments, her immemorial language, her changeless creed, her noble ritual, her stately ceremonies, her priceless works of art, her wondrous unity of doctrine, her ancient prayers, her matchless organization, her Apostolic authority, her splendid roll of Saints and Martyrs uniting earth and Heaven;

"When I reflect upon the intercession for us of those Saints and Martyrs, enhanced by the petitions of the Blessed Mother of Our Lord; and last but not least, when I consider the abiding Presence of the Savior on her altars—I feel this One, Holy, Apostolic Church has given me certainty for doubt, order for confusion, sunlight for darkness, and substance for shadow.

AN END TO DOUBT

"It is the Bread of Life and the Wine of the Soul, instead of unsatisfying husks; the father's welcome, with the ring and the robe, instead of the weary exile in the wilderness of doubt.

"It is true, the prodigal must retrace the homeward road, and even enter the doorway of the mansion on his knees. But within, what a recompense!

"Favored are those who, from their childhood up, are nurtured in the Catholic Church. Yet I have sometimes wondered whether such favored Catholics ever know the rapture of the homeless waif, to whom the splendors of his Father's house are suddenly revealed; the gratitude of the lonely wanderer, long lost in cold and darkness, who shares at last the warmth and light of God's great spiritual Home!"

Shortly after Stoddard and his wife joined the Church, he wrote a ten-stanza poem. Here are the first and last stanzas:

"Time-hallowed Church, whose truth divine
Endures unchanged from age to age,
What joy to feel that we are thine,
Nor lost our priceless heritage!

"Dear Mother Church, with grateful tears
We find the blessed fold of Rome,
Sad from the long past's wasted years,
But thankful to have reached our home."

CHAPTER FOUR—THE CATHOLIC CHURCH
SUPERIOR TO ALL CHURCHES

"The Catholic Church," said John L. Stoddard, "is the "Wonderful Body of the living Christ! In faith, in sacraments, in doctrine, in ceremonial, in language, in discipline, in its identical catechism, and in its one obedience to a single Head; in chapel, in cathedral, in hamlet, in metropolis, in Europe, Asia, Africa, America and on the islands of all seas, everywhere and at all times IT IS THE SAME!"

The Catholic Church is superior to all other churches not only because it was founded by Jesus Christ but because it alone has the Sacrifice of the Mass, offered in supreme adoration to God, which lifts our souls to Him as nothing else can do.

It is superior to all other churches because it alone has seven channels of grace, direct pipelines to God, instituted by Christ, which offer us a certainty of supernatural grace, giving us tranquility of conscience and peace of mind having an immense influence on our souls.

It is superior to all other churches because it alone stands for the idea that Ten Commandments, interpreted strictly, will count on judgment day toward salvation or damnation. All other religions seem to have blind spots for these commandments. A great many religions today allow their members to forget the commandment requiring weekly public worship of God, "Remember to keep holy the Sabbath day." Other religions, even strict ones such as Orthodox Judaism, allow divorce and remarriage, which Christ defined as adultery (Mt 5:19). No religion under God is free to dispense its members en masse from the Ten Commandments, or from any one of the Ten Commandments. If a religion ignores one of the commandments, or positively teaches that one of the commandments can be disobeyed, each of its members must disobey the religion, not the commandment. "If you wish to enter into life, keep the commandments," Christ said (Mt 19:17), and He interpreted the commandments much more strictly than the Pharisees did, who at the time were the leaders of the strictest religion on the face of the earth.

It is superior to all churches because it alone has the Holy Sacrament of the Eucharist in which Jesus Christ is really and substantially present under the appearance of bread: "Enter this door as if the floor within were gold; and every wall of jewels all of wealth untold; as if a choir in robes of fire were singing here; nor shout nor rush but hush – for God is here!"

These profound words by an anonymous poet express profoundly the unseen, incomprehensible, actual presence of Jesus Christ, God and Man, in the Catholic Church! Jesus is literally present in His Body, Blood, Soul and Divinity.

THE NEW TESTAMENT CAME LATER

In studying our religion, the first thing we should understand is that the Church Christ founded relies on far more than what the Gospel writers wrote down, brief as it was. The notion the Bible contains all Christ taught, or that it has all the answers to Christian living is not even claimed in the Bible.

Christ never wrote anything. He taught solely by the spoken word, and by example. He never told his Apostles to write down what they believed. He sent them to "teach all nations, preaching whatever I have commanded you" (Mk 28:20). Many years later, some of his disciples wrote down part of what they believed. But what they wrote provides only part of what He told them. Nor were they trying to teach history, or science.

When St. Paul mentioned in an epistle that "a little wine is good for the stomach," or "women should wear hats in church," he was not teaching about medicine, or about wearing hats for all time.

Christ founded His Church to lead and guide us. The Church produced the New Testament. The New Testament did not produce the Church! The New Testament did not come before the Church but later, from the Church.

The first generation of Christians did not have a New Testament. But they were the Church then, just as we are today. It was the Church that decided which Gospels, Epistles and other writings, such as the Acts of the Apostles, are authentic. That was not declared officially by the Church until 395 A.D.

By studying the New Testament we realize how joining the Church Christ founded is a community experience. Christ chose Peter and the other Apostles as the foundation of His Church. The history of twenty centuries convinces us that Peter and the other Apostles were succeeded by the bishop of Rome, and by the other bishops, and that the Church still has a universal shepherd, under Christ. That is why the Pope is called "the Vicar of Christ."

For many centuries the Church did not rely on Bible studies, apart from priests and scholars. Most people were illiterate, and printing was not invented until the 15th century. It used to take monks in monasteries an entire year to make a copy of the Bible by hand. When the Bible could be printed, it would be of little help to the illiterate masses.

After the Bible could be printed, the Church encouraged the faithful to read the Bible, particularly the New Testament, with the understanding that it is only a part of Christ's teaching. Much is contained in the teaching of the Church, which also explains the Bible, and in the writings of the Doctors of the Church, and in the lives of the Saints.

Every time we attend Mass we hear an Epistle and Gospel read, and a commentary by the priest explaining them. Every priest studies theology, and especially Sacred Scripture, for a minimum of four years, full time. He has been taught the official explanations of the Gospels.

INTERPRETING THE BIBLE

The idea that each person should rely on his or her own personal interpretation, independent of the Church's teaching, is fraught with error, confusion, and self-deception. The Bible is exciting to read, especially the New Testament. But the Church Christ founded is the official interpreter, and it teaches us far more than is contained in the brevity of the Gospels. No matter how much we rely on the Gospel, this must be kept in mind.

Regarding religious programs on the radio, for example, when callers ask questions, the person replying does not mention "private interpretation." He gives his opinion as the official one. For example, a caller recently asked a non-Catholic "expert" about Mary's comment: "From henceforth, all generations shall call me blessed" (Lk 1:48). The reply to the lady's question was: "Well, all generations will call you blessed, too, if you live right."

The whole idea of "private interpretation" implies that nothing is objective, that nothing is right or wrong. The idea of "private interpretation" is that Scripture means whatever you personally think it does, no matter what it really means—which makes no sense at all—and leads to a million errors. It is like taking two separate pieces of Scripture and running them together, e.g. "Judas went out and hung himself . . . Go thou and do likewise."

Christ never put up with error. He ridiculed the Pharisees and others when they interpreted His teachings incorrectly. The Apostles were so overwhelmed with the fact that Jesus was God that they sacrificed their lives to spread His message.

GROWTH OF THE CHURCH

In a *World News Report* issued May 6, 2000, Vatican City reported (Zenit.org): "The number of Catholics in the world has grown by 38% in the years of John Paul II's pontificate, according to the latest Statistical Yearbook of the Church.

"According to the yearbook, published by the *Libreria Editrice Vaticana,* the number of people baptized in the Catholic Church worldwide from 1978 to 2000 increased from 757 million to 1.045 billion.

"The numbers in Africa soared up by almost 140%. Europe is the last in this category, with 5.8% growth. In Asia, Catholics comprise only 2.9% of the population, in Europe it is 40%, in the Americas 63%, with peaks of 90.1% and 86.6% in the center and south of the continent, and 24.6% in the north.

"Over the 22-year period, the number of bishops has grown from 3,714 to 4,541, while priests total just over 405,000, down 3.75% from 1978. Diocesan clergy are growing everywhere, with some exceptions, whereas religious clergy are shrinking, except in Asia.

"Candidates for the priesthood, meanwhile, have soared from 64,000 in 1978 to 111,000 in 2000. Growth is notable in Asia and Africa, less so in Oceania, Europe and America.

"Permanent deacons have increased considerably everywhere since 1978, including a 678% rise in Europe. The ranks of professed male religious who are not priests have decreased notably, from 76,000 to just over 56,000.

"There has also been about a 19% decrease in professed women religious, though there is growth in the developing world."

The Catholic Church in the United States has quadrupled in size in the past three generations. And it is highly respected. One fourth of the members of the House and Senate are Catholic. So are about 90 percent of religious schools. The Catholic population in the U.S. is now 64 million, and increasing by more than a million members every year.

The continent of Africa, however, is even more surprising. In a country like Nigeria, for example, there were just 3,000 Catholics in 1902. Today there are 20 million Catholics in Nigeria alone, and vocations to the priesthood and convents are very flourishing. Yes, we have 64 million Catholics in our fifty states. But Africa has 85 million!

In many countries there, Sunday Masses last two hours each, as they begin with dancing and camaraderie, making it the social event of the week, as well as being very spiritual. It is common for the congregation to clap enthusiastically, hands held up to their faces, when the consecrated host, and then chalice, is held up. Priests from Africa are already helping staff parishes in many American dioceses.

Teaching scientific methods of agriculture and rural development is common in countries like Kenya, where Irish Franciscan Brothers staff agricultural colleges. It is reminiscent of how Benedictine monasteries in the Dark and Middle Ages taught the natives in Europe how to farm scientifically. Carrying on the teachings of the Church regarding spiritual values and family life is even more important, and more helpful. Devotion to the Mass, to the Sacred Heart of Jesus, and to the Rosary is practiced all over Africa.

CATHOLICISM VERSUS OTHER RELIGIONS

The power and authority to ordain successive bishops and priests has survived down the centuries through each Pope. The Catholic Church is the only one that maintained the power to consecrate bread and wine into Christ's body and blood. It is also the only Church that has kept the right of priests to forgive sins, adhering to Christ's promise to His first priests, the Apostles: "Whose sins you shall forgive, they are forgiven. Whose sins you shall retain [that are not forgiven], they are retained." These two great Sacraments are found only in the Catholic Church.

If you are a Roman Catholic, Jesus Christ, God and Man, began His – and your – Church in the year 33.

If you are Eastern Orthodox, your sect separated from Roman Catholicism around the year 1000.

If you are a Lutheran, your religion was founded by Martin Luther, an ex-monk of the Catholic Church, in 1517.

If you belong to the Church of England (Anglican), your religion was founded by King Henry VIII in the year 1534 because the pope would not grant him a divorce with the right to remarry.

If you are a Presbyterian, your religion was founded when John Knox brought the teachings of John Calvin to Scotland in the year 1560.

If you are a Unitarian, your religious group was founded by Theophilus Lindley, in London in the 1500s.

If you are a Congregationalist, your religion branched off from Puritanism in the early 1600s in England.

If you are a Baptist, you owe the tenets of your religion to John Smyth, who launched it in Amsterdam, Holland, in 1607.

If you are a Methodist, your religion was founded by John and Charles Wesley in England in 1744.

If you are an Episcopalian, your religion was brought over from England to the American colonies and formed a separate religion by Samuel Seabury in 1789.

If you are a Mormon (Latter Day Saints), Joseph Smith started your church in Palmyra, N.Y., not Salt Lake City, in the year 1830.

If you worship with the Salvation Army, your sect began with William Booth, in London in 1865.

If you are a Christian Scientist, you look to 1879 as the year your religion was founded by Mary Baker Eddy.

If you are a Jehovah's Witness, your religion was founded by Charles Taze Russell in Pennsylvania in the 1870s.

If you are a Pentecostal, your religion was started in the United States in 1901.

If you are an agnostic, you profess an uncertainty or a skepticism about the existence of God.

If you are an atheist, you do not believe in the existence of God.

If you are a member of the Jewish faith, your religion was founded by Abraham 4000 years ago.

If you are Hindu, your religion developed in India around 1,500 B.C..

If you are a Buddhist, your religion split from Hinduism, and was founded by Buddha, Prince of Siddhartha Gautama of India, about 500 B.C..

If you are Islamic, Mohammed started your religion in what is now Saudi Arabia around 600 A.D..

From the earliest centuries there were those who left the Catholic Church to start their own, usually because they disagreed with the teachings of the Church. The main religion that disagreed with Catholicism and does not recognize Christ as our Lord and Savior is the Church of Islam, known as Muslim, Moslem, and Mohammedanism. It is found almost universally among Arabs. But it has no one to head it, so it often gets involved in politics, in the name of religion. The rapid propagation of Mohammedanism is naturally explained. It flattered the passions and imposed itself by the sword. Christianity propagated itself in spite of passions and persecutions. Christianity should have perished if it had not been sustained by divine force.

Its founder, Mohammad (often spelled Muhammad) lived in Mecca (Saudi Arabia). He was born in 570 A.D., and died in 632. His father died before he was born, and his mother died when he was six years old. He became a trader and married a wealthy widow, whose financial affairs he managed. He later claimed the archangel Gabriel appeared to him, and told him he was a prophet.

He claimed the entire Koran, a book of 114 chapters and 510 pages, was revealed to him. Some accounts say the revelation was by the archangel Gabriel. Some say he said it was a direct revelation of God (whom his followers call Allah). It was the last revelation of God, he believed.

From the very beginning, Muhammad, who could neither read nor write, was involved in violence and political turmoil. He had opposition in Mecca, so he kept attacking innocent people with their trade caravans, simply to weaken the finances of the city of Mecca. There is no one or group in charge of Mohammedanism, so any of its followers can say they "disagree" with whatever other Mohammedans do.

Mohammedans constantly attack Christianity as "the infidel," and they are filled with hatred of Jews, as well, hating them as much as Hitler did. A Catholic pastor in the United States who came from India stated recently: "In that part of the world (referring to non-Christian areas) forgiveness is absolutely unknown."

40

Mohammedans ruling Sudan, for example, are constantly selling Christians there into slavery. Similarly, Mohammedans in the southern part of the Philippines keep kidnapping people in order to enrich themselves with millions of dollars in ransom. Such kidnappers sometimes kill their hostages, after ransom is paid.

The French are more correct than we think when they say: "In France we have one religion, but 200 sauces. In America, you have 200 religions, but only one sauce."

Voltaire was one of France's most clever writers. When the Huguenots asked him if he would like to attend their church, since he was not attending the Catholic Church very often, he replied: "I may have lost my faith, but not my reason." He also commented that "the Catholic Church is a hard Church to live in, but an easy Church to die in." However, to be certain of dying in the Catholic Church, we need to live in it. As Christ said, "Death may come like a thief in the night."

One of the greatest Church Councils, the Council of Trent, was held in three sessions from 1545 to 1563. It was held in response to the claims of Protestantism. A beautiful sentence from the Council refers to the Holy Eucharist: "In this Sacrament, God has poured forth bountifully the riches of His love." St. Peter Julian Eymard, who has been called "the Saint of the Eucharist," referred to the Blessed Sacrament in this way:

"It is the very culmination of His love. God can give no greater gift than Himself. By means of Communion, we receive Jesus Christ as God and Man, together with the merits of His mortal life and all its states, with the Redemption and all its fruits, even the pledge of future glory. We receive the greatest sum of happiness God can give on earth."

Father John Hardon, S.J., a very highly regarded theologian, gave this advice: "We should have Masses offered for our own intentions and for others, as the single most powerful source of supernatural blessings available to the human family."

He insisted that the Mass "is the principal channel of grace that we have. Prayer before the Blessed Sacrament," he pointed out "is indispensable to understand what we believe, and to know how we are to behave.

"The most fundamental reason why Christ is in the Holy Eucharist is to educate our minds to understand who He is: to penetrate into the meaning of the mysteries we believe; to understand how He wants us to live our lives."

He concluded: "Understanding the Eucharist is the greatest need in the Church today. The most wondrous mystery of our Catholic Faith is the Holy Eucharist. To believe in the Eucharist is to believe every other revealed mystery of Christianity."

We read in the writings of St. Ignatius, founder of the Jesuit Order: "To withdraw from creatures and repose with Jesus in the Tabernacle is my delight; there I can hide myself and seek rest. There I find a life which I cannot describe, a joy which I cannot make others comprehend, a peace such as is found only under the hospitable roof of our best Friend."

St. Francis of Assisi, the founder of the Franciscans, urged us "to show the greatest possible reverence and honor for the most holy Body and Blood of Our Lord Jesus Christ, through Whom all things, whether on the earth or in the heavens, have been brought to peace, and reconciled with Almighty God."

Charles Rich, the noted convert who spent many hours each day, as many as he could, before the Blessed Sacrament, commented:

"What is any church that does not offer us the sacramental presence of Jesus Christ? Is it not simply another building? What can any church offer us that does not offer us the Body, Blood, Soul and Divinity of Jesus Christ?"

CHAPTER FIVE—FOUND ONLY IN CATHOLICISM

Back in 1934, Fr. Wilfred H. Hurley, CSP, said: "Nineteen hundred years ago, with stern eyes, and words incisive and uncompromising, Jesus Christ warned men of the evils to come." But there was one evil which mankind should fear above all others. It was the evil Christ would warn them about again and again. Satan? Yes! But, Satan disguised as an angel of light!

"It is here! It is this evil which Christianity faces today! And the name of this horrific enemy is 'indifferentism!' You have heard the word. It is in the very atmosphere we breathe. People say it makes no difference what you believe, which church you attend, or if you pray. They say God doesn't care what you believe as long as you live a good life. This is a subtle attack on Christianity, and comes to us hand in hand with the material progress of our times. Through war, modern innovations, and vast travel, men have been thrown together in friendship, in fellowship, and in tolerance. The evil of indifference disguises itself, has spread worldwide, and threatens Christianity's very existence. Stop to consider: if one church is as good as another, then religion is reduced to a matter of sentiments and good taste. There is no truth in it. When you are indifferent to a thing, it does not require much opposition for you to give up that thing altogether. Religion is no exception. Fifty years ago, America was a Christian nation. Today at least 70% of the people state that they belong to no Church."

"One church," he continues, "is teaching 'this' set of rules, while another is teaching a different set, and yet a third has unique doctrines which absolutely contradict the other two. If the doctrine of one church is true, then the contradictory doctrines taught by another church, are false. If you say it makes no difference which church you attend, then you are blaspheming God, for by this you are saying that God is not a God of truth.

"Christ stood on trial before Pontius Pilot, and stated clearly, 'For this I was born, for this I came into the world: that I should give testimony to the truth.' If then, it makes no difference what you believe, then why did Christ suffer and die to establish the Catholic Church? Was He worse than a human fool? And what of the Apostles? Christ not only foresaw, but He even foretold the hardships, the persecution, and the cruel deaths His faithful followers would undergo. Could Jesus Christ give such a command to us, and yet be a loving God? He knew that His martyrs would be bodily torn limb from limb, have their ears cut off, their eyes burned with hot coals, their tongues ripped out, and red hot lead poured down their throats. Can you picture Christ, then, His lips curled in mocking derision, saying, *I was only joking! It really makes no difference what you believe, or if you believe anything at all. The joke is on you!*" Is such a thing even imaginable? NO! Yet it is this picture which is painted by ndifferentism! Indifferentism is nothing but blasphemy! It is nothing more than Atheism disguised as fellowship, tolerance, and friendship. Can you not see that it is a denunciation of Christ? That it makes fools of all Christians."

"No intelligent and reasoning man or woman," he adds, "can hold to indifferentism. For the glory of our Father, and our eternal happiness, God demands that each of us belong to the One True Church which He came to earth and gave His life to found. The dogma, doctrine, and traditions of this Church are to be taught to all nations for all times. It is to this Church that we must belong. *One Church is not as good as another!"*

It was this great presence of the Body of Christ in the Blessed Sacrament, found only in Catholicism, that gave John Cardinal Henry Newman the courage and strength required to take the biggest step in his life! In fact, because of Christ's presence, Newman saw the necessity for all unbelievers to return to the bosom of the Catholic Church, which he termed the "True Fold."

Cardinal Newman is one of the great literary figures in the English language. College students are familiar with Catholic headquarters on secular campuses as "The Newman Center." We often hear or read of "Cardinal Newman," but tend to forget he had to leave the church of his birth, Anglicanism, to become Catholic in 1845. At that time, Catholicism had been ruthlessly persecuted in England for nearly 200 years.

When Newman became a Catholic he suffered greatly. He was one of the most popular preachers and writers in the Anglican Church. People came from all parts of England to hear him preach. Because he was so gifted a thinker and writer, his sermons and pamphlets were read far and wide. In mid-life, because of his scholarly study, his love of truth made him become a Catholic. He was now scorned by those who had loved him. His friends turned against him, and he had to resign from his position as a professor, losing his source of income. His move, he said, "was like going out on an open sea." But he was sustained by the presence of Christ in the Blessed Sacrament.

He noted: "It is such an incomprehensible blessing to have Christ in bodily presence in one's house, within one's wall, that it swallows up all other privileges and destroys, or should destroy, every pain. It is really most wonderful," he continued, "to see the Divine Presence looking out almost into the open streets from the various Churches . . . I never knew what worship was, as an objective fact, till I entered the Catholic Church."

He also wrote, by way of explanation: "We call His presence in this Holy Sacrament a spiritual presence, not as if 'spiritual' were but a name or mode of speech, and He were really absent, but by way of expressing that He who is present there can neither be seen nor heard; that He cannot be approached or ascertained by any of the senses; that He is not present in any way we know, though He is really present. And how this is, of course, is a mystery."

After all his studies, Newman wrote: "To go deeply into history is to cease to be a Protestant." A stunning example is the inscription on British coins: DF, which stands for "Defensor Fidei," "Defender of the Faith." But it refers to a title conferred on Henry VIII by the Pope for defending the Catholic Church with his book on the Seven Sacraments, before he broke away from the Church. The Queen and Protestant leaders in England do not want to admit this. They ignore history, and in fact, they don't like to think that Henry VIII, who killed several of his wives out of concupiscence to marry another, was really the founder of their religion.

Some even try to say it was founded by St. Thomas the Apostle. But if so, why did Henry try to get the Pope to approve his divorce? The records in the Vatican make it very clear that the Church in England was under the Popes until 1534, when Henry broke away. Even he was confused, and he left money in his will to have Masses offered for his soul.

Another feature in King Henry's career was when he sentenced Thomas More to death for not accepting the King's second marriage. More was imprisoned in the Tower of London. The King wrote him that since More had been knighted by the Crown, Speaker of the House of Commons, the first layman to be Lord Chancellor, and had been such a close friend of the King for so many years, after his head was to be chopped off, his body would not be cut into four quarters. More commented from prison that he hoped not many of the king's friends "would be treated with such kindness." No wonder Anglicans don't take pride in their Church's founder.

Compare the rational of Martin Luther with that of the great St. Paul. Chastity, Luther declared, was unnatural; celibacy was a sin; Sacraments were profitless; the Mass was idolatrous; there was no longer any need of examining one's conscience or of going to confession; and the Pope was Antichrist! Faith alone, he said, was essential to salvation; good works were unnecessary. What a contrast between Luther's words and the great Apostle Paul who wrote: "I see another law in my members, warring against the law of my mind and bringing me into captivity to the law of sin, which is in my members. O wretched man that I am! Who shall deliver me from the body of this death? And "They that are Christ's have crucified the flesh with the affections and lusts." And again, "If you live by the flesh, you shall die; but if you, through the Spirit, do mortify the deeds of the body, you shall live."

A well known philosopher, Dr. von Hartmann, in comparing the Catholic Church with Protestantism, says: "If it is a Church that is to bring me to salvation

. . then I will look about me for a firmly established, powerful Church, and I prefer to cling to the Rock of Peter, rather than to any one of the numberless Protestant sectarian churches."

OTHERS WERE MAKING THE SAME JOURNEY

When Avery Dulles went to Harvard, he found Protestantism had little to offer. After studying the early Fathers of the Church such as Augustine, St. Bernard and Thomas Aquinas, as well as Dante and others, he also studied the writings of Luther, Calvin and other Reformers. Avery compared them with the Council of Trent, and found his sympathies were always on the Catholic side. He also studied modern Catholic writers like Maritain and Gilson, and found them "full of light."

Avery found his philosophy professors at Harvard had great esteem for Catholic philosophers. He himself found such writings "extremely helpful in applying Christian principles to the modern world in all spheres, from aesthetics all the way to politics and international affairs."

Even more, said Avery recently, "The Catholic Church had a hold on its people that no Protestant church seemed to have. He noticed that Catholics "were attending church services in huge numbers, including Confession, Communion, Benediction, Holy Week services, and other spiritual events. I was also attracted in many ways to the liturgy.

"It was a combination of all those factors, without much personal contact with individual Catholics, that led me into the Catholic Church. It was a kind of solitary journey; then I later discovered that others were making the same journey, though I did not realize it at the time."

He then wrote his parents that he planned to become a Catholic. When he went to New York it was his father who saw that he had thought it through very carefully. The father finally said, "Well, you're an adult, you can make your own decisions." Avery explained that for him it was a matter of conscience.

In a few years Avery Dulles entered the Jesuit Order. He later taught philosophy and theology. Over the years he has written more than thirty books on theology and so distinguished himself that Pope John Paul II made him a Cardinal in 2001, without his ever having served as a bishop.

Cardinal Dulles teaches theology in the graduate school at Fordham University in New York, at the age of 81. His theology is so accurate and so inspiring, that the Holy Father wanted him to be the theological teacher and writer all other theologians could look up to. There was no better way for the Vatican to endorse his very sound theology than to make him a Cardinal, the highest position in the Church next to the Pope.

In theology, humility is defined as truth. In his own humble way, Cardin Avery Dulles continues his research, and his priceless theological writing and teaching. Of the countless converts to the Church in the past century, only Cardinal Newman in England compared with Avery Dulles, two very distinguished and dedicated scholars who contributed so much to the Church of their adoption.

MORE THAN A BILLION MEMBERS

When one of England's greatest historians, Thomas Babington Macaulay, wrote about the history of Roman Catholicism, he described the Church as the greatest organization the world has ever seen. He was not a Catholic, and Catholicism was very much suppressed in England at the time he wrote, in the 1840's.

Macaulay served more than 20 years in the House of Commons, four of which he spent in India, where he modeled its educational system on that of England. When Macaulay was asked to write a preface to a history of the Papacy, he made an intense study of Catholicism. This is what he wrote of the Catholic Church, as a profound scholar and historian:

"There is not, and there never was on this earth, a work of human policy so well deserving of examination as the Roman Catholic Church. The history of that Church joins together the two great ages of human civilization.

"No other institution is left standing which carries the mind back to the times when the smoke of sacrifice rose from the Pantheon, and when tigers bounded in the Flavian amphitheater.

"The proudest royal houses are but of yesterday, when compared with the line of the Supreme Pontiffs. That line we trace back in an unbroken series from the Pope who crowned Napoleon in the nineteenth century to the Pope who crowned Pepin in the eighth; and far beyond the time of Pepin the august dynasty extends, till it is lost in the twilight of fable.

"The republic of Venice came next in antiquity. But the republic of Venice was modern when compared with the Papacy; and the republic of Venice is gone, and the Papacy remains. The Papacy remains, not in decay, but full of life and useful vigor.

"The Catholic Church is still sending forth to the farthest ends of the world missionaries as zealous as those who landed in Kent with Augustin, and still confronting hostile kings with the same spirit with which she confronted Attila.

"The number of her children is greater than in any former age. Her acquisitions in the New World have more than compensated for what she has lost in the Old. Her spiritual ascendancy extends over the vast countries which 'e between the planes of the Missouri and Cape Horn, countries which, a century

47

Эnce, may not improbably contain a population as large as that which now ЭПhabits Europe.

"The members of her communion are certainly not fewer than a hundred and fifty millions; and it will be difficult to show that all other Christian sects united amount to a hundred and twenty millions. Nor do we see any sign which indicates that the term of her long dominion is approaching.

"She saw the commencement of all the governments and of all the ecclesiastical establishments that now exist in the world; and we feel no assurance that she is not destined to see the end of them all.

"She was great and respected before the Saxon had set foot on Britain, before the Frank had passed the Rhine, when Grecian eloquence still flourished in Antioch, when idols were still worshipped in the temple of Mecca.

"And she may still exist in undiminished vigor when some traveler from New Zealand shall, in the midst of a vast solitude, take his stand on a broken arch of London Bridge to sketch the ruins of St. Paul's."

(St. Paul's in London is the main church built by Protestantism in England. Westminster Abbey and so many other Protestant churches in England were built before Henry VIII broke away from Rome and started the Church of England, known as the Anglican Church there, and as the Episcopal Church in America). Anglicanism is still the official government religion in England, and Catholics are just ten percent of the population. But more than half of the people who attend church in England on Sunday are Roman Catholics. Countless Anglican churches have been torn down, or turned into commercial buildings.

There are less practicing Protestants today throughout the world than the one hundred and twenty million Macaulay estimated in the 1840's. The number of Catholics in the world, by contrast, has increased seven hundred percent, to more than a billion. And the number increases every year. In Macaulay's time, for example, there were just a few thousand Catholics in Africa. Today there are eighty-five million.

There are two main reasons why the number of Catholics keeps increasing every year: 1) Catholicism is the Church Christ founded; 2) It concentrates on the Holy Sacrifice of the Mass, as Christ insisted that His followers should do: the renewal of Calvary, "in remembrance of me."

In 1919, the Rev. Robert Westly Peach of Newark, N.J., in a report which he submitted to the Interchurch Council on Organic Union, which met in Philadelphia, stated that Protestants in America had built perhaps 100,000 unnecessary churches at a cost of $500,000,000. "The Roman churches," he says, "are crowded; ours, on an average, less than one-quarter filled."

CHAPTER SIX—DIVISION

Just as there is but one Constitution – and not fifty individual Constitutions – drawn up for the fifty individual States of America, so too Christianity correctly and completely presented cannot signify a multitude of sects – blending isolated truths of the Christian religion, with errors which form the basis of division – among themselves.

George Washington and the founding fathers drew up but one constitution to be followed by all Americans; Christ with the Apostles established but one Church to be followed by all Christians.

Christ insisted that unity would be an outstanding characteristic of His Church. The unity of Catholicism is certainly as striking as is its absence in Protestantism. And the divisions have been taking place continuously throughout the almost 500 years since the Reformation. They cannot all be teaching the truth.

Although now divided into many hundreds of denominations, the original families of Protestantism were five: the Lutheran, Calvanist, Zwinglian, Anglican and Congregational. Their three basic beliefs are:

1) The Bible is the only rule of faith, excluding tradition and Church Authority.

2) Justification by faith alone, excluding supernatural merit and good works.

3) The universal priesthood of believers, excluding a distinct priesthood.

There is at work in Protestantism a process of disintegration, which apparently nothing can check; for all these humanly created sects originate from the notion that dissatisfied members of a church have a right to leave it and found another, which they call "reformed" – all of which are "reformations" of other "reformations" of the original Luther's "Reformation!"

In the August/September issue, 2002, of *Homiletic and Pastoral Review*, page 48, this statement is printed: "'Today, there is a new religion starting every five days.' These statistics have been gathered by former Protestant Ministers who have converted to the Catholic Faith."

The inability of Protestants to agree among themselves proves that Protestantism is a false system; for every Protestant church that teaches one doctrine, there is a Protestant church that denies it. And because the Protestant churches owe their existence to the fact that each denies that the others really know what Scripture means, there is not a Protestant church – instead, there are hundreds of different brands of Protestantism.

Christ promised that His Church would not fail; Protestant reformers said that it did fail. Just as no ordinary citizen has the right to enter a court and declare himself a judge, so too no man has the right to set up new churches or new doctrines.

Rev. Dr. Goudge, Professor of Anglican theology, has stated, "The New Testament absolutely requires Church unity. The various sects have adopted isolated aspects of Christianity. But Dr. Goudge says that "Christianity *a la cart* will not do. The religion of Christ must be accepted or rejected as a whole."

Rev. Dr. Briggs, a Presbyterian scholar, says that, "while there can be a unity of the Christian spirit without unity of authority, there can be no Church unity without unity of authority."

Robert Hugh Benson, the son of a former Archbishop of Canterbury, became a Catholic. In his book, *Christ in the Church,* he writes: "It is impossible to make men of one nation agree even on political matters. Yet the Catholic Church makes men of all nations agree on religion doctrines. When I was a student at Cambridge, I often used to find in one lecture hall, men of one nation and six religions. When I became a student in the University of Rome, I found in the one room, men of six nations and one religion. Is it conceivable that it is a merely human power that makes such a thing possible?"

Christ, being God, possessed wisdom and knowledge in an infinite degree. With Him there could be no such thing as aimless intention or wasted effort. He had a definite goal for everything He did. He came to save souls; therefore, he would not have created such confusion by founding many churches with conflicting doctrines. He foresaw and predicted such divisions. "There will arise false Christs," He said, "to deceive if possible even the elect" (Mt 24:24).

A PROCESS OF DISINTEGRATION

Christ said of His Church: "The gates of Hell shall not prevail against it" (Mt 16:18). In alphabetical order, here is what the gates of Hell did with the Protestant churches, by prevailing against them since their break in 1517:

Advent Christians
Adventists
African Methodist Episcopal
African Methodist Episcopal Zion
African Union Protestant
Age-to-Come Adventists
American Episcopal Church
Amish Mennonites

Anabaptists
Apostolic Mennonites
Arminian Baptists
Associate Kirk
Associate Presbyterian, North America
Associate Reform Presbyterian
Associate Reform of the South
Bible Christians
British Methodist Episcopal
British Wesleyans
Calvinistic Baptists
Cameronians
Campbellite Baptists
Christadelphians
Christian Disciples
Christian Eliasites
Christian Israelites
Christ-ians
Christian Scientists
Church of God
Church of God Adventists
Church of the Living God
Church of Progress
Church of Scotland in England
Coarse Mennonites
Colored Methodist Episcopal
Congregationalists
Congregation Methodist
Countess of Huntington's Connexion
Covenanters
Cumberland Presbyterian Church (colored)
Cumberland Presbyterian Church (white)
Disciples of Christ
Dowieites
Dunkard Brethren
Eastern Reformed Presbyterian
Evangelical Adventists
Evangelical Association
Evangelicals
Evangelical Unionists

51

Evangelical Missionary
Family of Love
Free Church of England
Free Kirk of Scotland
Free Methodist
Free-Will Baptists
General Baptists
General Baptists, New Connexion
General Conference Mennonites
Hicksite Quakers
Hyper-Calvinists
Independent Methodists
Irvingites
Jezreelites
Life and Advent Union
Lutherans (many varieties)
Mennonites (plain)
Methodist Church, Canada
Methodist Episcopal
Methodist Episcopal, South
Methodist Protestant
Methodists
Millerites
Moravians
Mormons (Latter Day Saints)
New Connexion Methodists
Old Amish Mennonites
Old Church of Scotland
Old Mennonites
Original Seceders
Orthodox Quakers
Other Mennonites
Padeo-Baptists
Particular Baptists
Pentecostal Dancers
Pillars of Fire
Plymouth Brethren
Presbyterian Baptists
Presbyterians
Primitive Baptists

Primitive Friends Quakers
Protestant Episcopal Church
Refined Mennonites
Reformed Episcopal Church
Reformed Mennonites
Reformed Presbyterian Church
Reformed Presbyterian Covenant
Reformed Presbyterians
Reformed Zwinglians
Reform Kirk
Reform Union Methodists
Regular Mennonites
Relief Kirk
River Brethren
Salvation Army
Schwenckfeldians
Secession Church of Ireland
Secession Kirk
Separate Baptists
Seventh Day Adventists
Seventh Day Baptists
Shakers
Six Principal Baptists
Socinians
Spiritualists
Temperance Methodists
The Agapemone
The Apostolics
The Baptised Believers
The Benevolent Methodists
The Bible Defence Association
The Brethren
The Bryanites
The Church of England, Broad
The Church of England, High
The Church of England, Low
The Eclectics
The Followers of the Lord Jesus Christ
The Free Christians
The Free Evangelical Christians

The Five Gospel Brethren
The Free Gospellers
The Free Grace Gospel Christians
The Glassites
The Glory Band
The Hallelujah Band
The Holy Ghost and Us Society
The Holy Jumpers
The Hope Mission
The Humanitarians
The Inghamites
Theistic Church
The Kihamites
The Muggleltonians
The New Wesleyans
The Old Baptists
The Open Baptists
The Peculiar People
The Primitive Congregation
The Primitive Methodists
The Progressionists
The Protestant Trinitarians
The Ranters
The Rational Christians
The Recreative Religionists
The Salem Society
The Secularists
The Separatists
The Spiritual Church
The Strict Baptists
The Union Baptists
The United Christian Church
Unification Church (Moonies)
Unitarian Baptists
Unitarians
United American Methodist Episcopal
United Baptists
United Brethren
United Brethren in Christ
United Free Gospel Methodists

United Free Methodists
United Presbyterian, North America
United Presbyterians
Universalists
Wesleyan Methodists
Welsh Calvinistic
Wilburite Quakers
Zion Union Apostolic
Zwinglians

THEY WILL NOT ENDURE SOUND DOCTRINE

St. Paul warned, "There shall be a time when they will not endure sound doctrine; but, according to their own desires, they will heap to themselves teachers, having itching ears; and will indeed turn away their hearing from the truth, but will be turned unto fables" (2 Tim 4:3-4).

A perfect example of what St. Paul was speaking of is that of the Moonies – one of the most recent churches to proclaim itself the true church. In their monthly flyer, August 2002, Report 21, *Miles Christi,* carried the following article:

"Expansion of the Moonies. Do you know who Sun Myung Moon is? He is the founder and leader of the so-called Unification Church, better known as the Moonies. He was born in North Korea in 1920, son of Protestant Presbyterian peasants. In 1945 he proclaimed himself to be the Messiah and founded his first church. He officially founded his sect in 1954, calling it the *'Association of the Holy Spirit for the Unification of world-wide Christianity.'*

"He was imprisoned in Korea for adultery and immorality. In 1973 he settled in the USA reportedly because it "possesses 60% of the wealth of the world." He was imprisoned in 1984 for tax evasion, although he ably gained some profit in proselytism from his prison. He was married four times, the last time in his forties with an eighteen year old "new Eve," with whom he has had 14 children.

"What is the Church of the Unification? It is a powerful economic empire, operating with banks and financial institutions, communications media, especially the press, real estate, and with strong ties to the naval industry and arms traffic. In the past decade, he has made attempts to penetrate into Catholic and military circles. The case of Archbishop Milingo is a recent example. His proselytism aims at recruiting important figures with economic influence. According to his publications, the sect is present in 130 countries and in 1990 had about three million members.

55

"His doctrine is a collage of a mixture of the Bible and his own fantasy, xpounded in his dense work, *The Divine Principles* (1957). He holds that since Adam and Jesus Christ have failed, he himself, Moon, is the savior of the world. According to this savior, God will send the lord of the Second Coming before the end of the century, as a third attempt to set up his kingdom on earth, which will finally be established. He has organized a system of propaganda and proselytism with rigorous discipline, especially among the young. Marriage among his adepts must have his approval and blessing, and he has the final word on the choice of spouses. The children of these unions, celebrated en masse, are said to be born without original sin."

CHAPTER SEVEN—UNITY

Christ founded a Church and said that the gates of hell would never prevail against it. He also said that He would be with it all days until the end of the world. His Church, therefore, must still be in this world, and must have been in the world every day since He founded it. That rules out all other churches except the Catholic Church; for all other churches came into existence long after Christ. It is impossible to believe that Christ, Truth itself, and infinite Wisdom, taught such contradictory doctrines and obligations.

God must be partial to the doctrine taught by His own Son Jesus, and He cannot be indifferent to blasphemous denials of the veracity of Christ. And God must be partial to the exact and complete teachings of Christ, and not to incomplete or distorted teachings proposed by men who, with no authority to do so, tampered with the teachings of Christ. If you are honest enough to admit this, you admit that God is partial to the Catholic Church, and that He is not pleased with other churches which cannot agree among themselves except in their opposition to the greatest Church of all – the Catholic Church!

"If a man will not hear the Church, let him be as the heathen" (Mt 18:17). There is therefore a Church to which we must submit if we wish to belong to Christ. Which is that Church? It is the Catholic Church which is the only Church that goes back to the time of Christ.

CHRIST NEVER NAMED HIS CHURCH

Christ never named His Church so that false churches could not claim it as their church. Instead He gave it four distinctive characteristics that no other church has, or can possibly copy. These marks declare the Church to be the true faith and the instrument of salvation. It is the one Church in the world, founded by and belonging completely to Christ, as opposed to other rival churches of Christianity claiming to be the true church. These four marks were first enumerated by the First Council of Constantinople in the year 381.

(1) The Church is one because its members are united in faith and doctrine, under the pope.

(2) The Church is holy because it offers the means of sanctifying grace and because it was founded by Christ and is animated by the Holy Spirit.

(3) The Church is Catholic (meaning universal) because it is intended for all peoples in all places of the world.

(4) The Church is apostolic because of the unbroken line from the apostles to the bishops whose teaching authority, the Magisterium, can be traced to the eternal and unquestionable teachings of Christ.

Jesus Christ established one religion; He wanted it to be preached in its entirety to all peoples of the earth, to endure until the end of time and to be embraced by all men. Reason tells us that it would not be possible to have several true Churches. A Church, in order to be true, must teach the pure doctrine of Jesus Christ. Since that truth is necessarily one, only one true Church can be found among those that possess contrary doctrines.

DIVINE TITLE, DEED, & ABSTRACT OF THE CATHOLIC CHURCH

Only the Catholic Church claims Christ as both its divine Founder and its Head. All other religious denominations claim Christ as their head but they admit that a man is their founder!

Christ did not say: "You are Peter, and upon this rock I will build my Churches, and the gates of Hell shall not prevail against them!" Christ said: "And I say unto you, you are Peter, and upon this rock I will build my Church, and the gates of Hell shall not prevail against it" (Mt 16:18).

As long as he lived, St. Peter was the head of the Church. The bishops that he established were invested with the dignity but not with the leadership of the Church, which he kept until his death. When he died, his successor inherited his title of Bishop of Rome and also the power of head of the Church, just as a prince, who succeeds a king, inherits all the authority with which he had been invested.

All the Popes have been recognized as head of the Church. They were consulted from all sides, and they proclaimed laws for the entire Church, presided over councils, condemned heretics and deposed unworthy bishops.

The Pope is the head of the Church of Jesus Christ since we cannot say, without denying the divinity of Jesus Christ, that He has failed to keep His promise to preserve the foundation of His Church until the end of time. Here is the unbroken line of Popes, their birthplace or country of origin, and the years of their reign for twenty one centuries:

1. St. Peter: Bethsaida in Galilee, 67
2. St. Linus, Tuscany, 67-76
3. St. Anacletus, Rome, 76-88
4. St. Clement I, Rome, 88-97
5. St. Evaristus, Greece, 97-105
6. St. Alexander I, Rome, 105-115
7. St. Sixtus I, Rome, 115-125
8. St. Telesphorus, Greece, 125-136
9. St. Hyginus, Greece, 136-140
10. St. Pius I, Aquileia, 140-155

11. St. Anicetus, Syria, 155-166
12. St. Soter, Campania, 166-175
13. St. Eleutherius, Nicopolis in Epirus, 175-189
14. St. Victor I, Africa, 189-199
15. St. Zephyrinus, Rome, 199-217
16. St. Callistus I, Rome, 217-222
17. St. Urban I, Rome, 222-230
18. St. Pontian, Rome, July 21, 230, to Sept. 28, 235
19. St. Anterus, Greece, Nov. 21, 235, to Jan. 3, 236
20. St. Fabian, Rome, Jan. 10, 236, to Jan. 20, 250
21. St. Cornelius, Rome, Mar. 251, to June 253
22. St. Lucius I,Rome; June 25, 253, to Mar. 5, 254
23. St. Stephen I, Rome, May 12, 254, to Aug. 2, 257
24. St. Sixtus II, Greece, Aug. 30, 257 to Aug. 6, 258
25. St. Dionysius, July 22, 259, to Dec. 26, 268
26. St. Felix I, Rome, Jan. 5, 269, to Dec. 30, 274
27. St. Eutychian, Luni, Jan. 4, 275 to Dec. 7, 283
28. St. Caius, Dalmatia, Dec. 17, 283, to Apr. 22, 296
29. St. Marcillinus, Rome, June 30, 296, to May. 25, 304
30. St. Marcellus I, Rome, Oct. 27, 304, to Jan. 16, 309
31. St. Eusebius, Greece, Apr. 18, 309 to Aug. 17, 311
32. St. Melchiades, (Miltiades): Africa; July 2, 311, to Jan. 11, 314
33. St. Sylvester I, Rome, Jan. 31, 314, to Dec. 31, 335
34. St. Marcus, Rome, Jan. 18, 336, to Oct. 7, 336
35. St. Julius I, Rome, Feb. 6, 337, to Apr. 12, 352
36. St. Liberius, Rome, May 17, 352, to Sept. 24, 366
37. St. Damasus I, Spain, Oct. 1, 366, to Dec. 11, 384
38. St. Siricius, Rome, Dec. 15, 384, to Nov. 26, 399
39. St. Anastasius I, Rome, Nov. 27, 399, to Dec. 19, 401
40. St. Innocent I, Albano, Dec. 22, 401, to Mar. 12, 417
41. St. Zosimus, Greece, Mar. 18, 417, to Dec. 26, 418
42. St. Boniface 1, Rome, Dec. 28, 418, to Sept. 4, 422
43. St. Celestine I, Campania, Sept. 10, 422, to July 27, 432
44. St. Sixtus III, Rome, July 31, 432, to Aug. 19, 440
45. St. Leo I (the Great), Tuscany, Sept. 29. 440, to Nov. 10, 461
46. St. Hilarius, Sardinia, Nov. 19, 461, to Feb. 29, 468
47. St. Simplicius, Tivoli, Mar. 3, 468, to Mar. 10, 483
48. St. Felix II, Rome, Mar. 13, 483, to Mar. 1, 492
49. St. Gelasius I, Africa, Mar. 1, 492, to Nov. 21, 496
50. Anastasius II, Rome, Nov. 24, 496, to Nov. 19, 498

51. St. Symmachus, Sardinia, Nov. 22, 498, to July 19, 514
52. St. Hormisdas, Frosinone, July 20, 514, to Aug. 6, 523
53. St. John I, Martyr, Tuscany, Aug. 13, 523, to May 18, 526
54. St. Felix III, Samnium, July 12, 526, to Sept. 22, 530
55. Boniface II, Rome, Sept. 22, 530, to Oct. 17, 532
56. John II, Rome, Jan. 2, 533, to May 8, 535
57. St. Agapitus I, Rome, May 13, 535, to Apr. 22, 536
58. St. Silverius, Campania, June 1, 536, to Nov. 11, 537
59. Vigilius, Rome, Mar. 29, 537, to June 7, 555
60. Pelagius I, Rome, Apr. 16, 556, to Mar. 4, 561
61. John III, Rome, July 17, 561, to July 13, 574
62. Benedict I, Rome, June 2, 575, to July 30, 579
63. Pelagius II, Rome, Nov. 26, 579, to Feb. 7, 590
64. St. Gregory I, (the Great), Rome, Sept. 3, 590, to Mar. 12, 604
65. Sabinianus, Blera in Tuscany, Sept. 13, 604, to Mar. 12, 606
66. Boniface III, Rome, Feb. 19, 607, to Nov. 12, 607
67. St. Boniface IV, Abruzi, Aug. 25, 608, to May 8, 615
68. St. Deusdedit, Rome, Oct. 19, 615, to Nov. 8, 618
69. Boniface V, Naples, Dec. 23, 619, to Oct. 25, 625
70. Honorius I, Campania, Oct. 27, 625, to Oct. 12, 638
71. Severinus, Rome, May 28, 638, to Aug. 2, 640
72. John IV, Dalmatia, Dec. 24, 640, to Oct. 12, 642
73. Theodore I, Greece, Nov. 24, 642, to May 14, 649
74. St. Martin I, Martyr, todi, July 1, 649, to Sept. 16, 655
75. St. Eugene I, Rome, Nov. 10, 655, to June 2, 657
76. St. Vitalian, Segni, July 30, 657, to Jan. 27, 672
77. Adeodatus, Rome, Apr. 11, 672, to June 17, 676
78. Donus, Rome, Nov. 2, 676, to Apr. 11, 678
79. St. Agatho, Sicily, June 27, 678, to Jan 10. 681
80. St. Leo II, Sicily, Aug. 17, 682, to July 3, 683
81. St. Benedict II, Rome, June 26, 684, to May 8, 685
82. John V, Syria, July 23, 685, to Aug. 2, 686
83. Conon, birth place unknown, Oct. 21, 686, to Sept. 21, 687
84. St. Sergius I, Syria, Dec. 15, 687, to Sept. 8, 701
85. John VI, Greece, Oct. 30, 701, to Jan 11, 705
86. John VII, Greece, Mar. 1, 705, to Oct. 18, 707
87. Sisinnius, Syria, Jan. 15, 708, to Feb. 4, 708
88. Constantine, Syria, Mar. 25, 708, to Apr. 9, 715
89. St. Gregory II, Rome, May 19, 715, to Feb. 11, 731
90. St. Gregory III, Syria, Mar. 18, 731, to Nov. 1, 741

91. St. Zacharias, Greece, Dec. 10, 741, to Mar. 22, 752
92. Stephen II, Rome, Mar. 26, 752, to Apr. 26, 757
93. St. Paul I, Rome, May 29, 757, to June 28, 767
94. Stephen III, Sicily, Aug. 1, 768, to Jan. 24, 772
95. Adrian I, Rome, Feb. 1, 772, to Dec. 25, 795
96. St. Leo III, Rome, Dec. 26, 795, to June 12, 816
97. Stephen IV, Rome, June 22, 816, to Jan. 24, 817
98. St. Paschal I, Rome, Jan. 25, 817, to Feb. 11, 824
99. Eugene II, Rome, Feb. 2, 824, to Aug. 5, 827
100. Valentine, Rome, Aug. 827 to Sept. 827
101. Gregory IV, Rome, Oct. 827 to Jan. 844
102. Sergius II, Rome, Jan. 844 to Jan. 27, 847
103. St. Leo IV, Rome, Apr. 10, 847 to July 17, 855
104. Benedict III, Rome, Sept. 29, 855 to Apr. 17, 858
105. St. Nicholas I, (the Great), Rome, Apr. 24, 858, to Nov. 13, 867
106. Adrian II, Rome, Dec. 14, 867, to Dec. 14, 872
107. John VIII, Rome, Dec. 14, 872, to Dec. 16, 882
108. Marinus I, Gallese, Dec. 16, 882, to May 15, 884
109. St. Adrian III, Rome, May 17, 884, to Sept. 6, 885
110. Stephen V, Rome, Sept. 885 to Sept. 14, 891
111. Formosus, Porto, Oct. 6, 891, to Apr. 4, 896
112. Boniface VI, Rome, Apr. 896 to Apr. 896
113. Stephen VI, Rome, May 896 to Aug. 897
114. Romanus, Gallese, Aug. 897 to Nov. 897
115. Theodore II, Rome, Dec. 897 to Dec. 897
116. John IX, Tivoli, Jan. 898 to Jan. 900
117. Benedict IV, Rome, Jan. 900 to July 903
118. Leo V, Ardea, July 903 to Sept. 903
119. Sergius III, Rome, Jan. 29, 904, to Apr. 14, 911
120. Anastasius III, Rome, Apr. 911 to June 913
121. Lando, Sabina, July 913 to Feb. 914
122. John X, Tossignana (Imola), Mar. 914 to May 928
123. Leo VI, Rome, May 928 to Dec. 928
124. Stephen VII, Rome, Dec. 928 to Feb. 931
125. John XI, Rome, Feb. 931 to Dec. 935
126. Leo VII, Rome, Jan. 3, 936, to July 13, 939
127. Stephen VIII, Rome, July 14, 939, to Oct. 942
128. Marinus II, Rome, Oct. 30, 942, to May 946
129. Agapitus II, Rome, May 10, 946, to Dec. 955
130. John XII, Tusculum, Dec. 16, 955, to May 14, 964

131.	Leo VIII, Rome, Dec. 4, 964, to Mar. 1, 965
132.	Benedict V, Rome, 965
133.	John XIII, Rome, Oct. 1, 965, to Sept. 6, 972
134.	Benedict VI, Rome, Jan. 19, 973, to June 974
135.	Benedict VII, Rome, Oct. 974 to July 10, 983
136.	John XIV, Pavia, Dec. 983 to Aug. 20, 984
137.	John XV, Rome, Aug. 985 to Mar. 996
138.	Gregory V, Saxony, May 3, 996, to Feb. 18, 999
139.	Sylvester II, Auvergne, Apr. 2, 999, to May 12, 1003
140.	John XVII, Rome, June 1003 to Dec. 1003
141.	John XVIII, Rome, Jan. 1004 to July 1009
142.	Sergius IV, Rome, July 31, 1009, to May 12, 1012
143.	Benedict VIII, Tusculum, May 18, 1012, to Apr. 9, 1024
144.	John XIX, Tusculum, Apr. 1024 to 1032
145.	Benedict IX, Tusculum, 1032 to 1044
146.	Sylvester III, Rome, Jan 20, 1045, to Feb. 10, 1045
147.	Benedict IX, (second time), Apr. 1045, to May 1, 1045
148.	Gregory VI, Rome, May 5, 1045, to Dec. 20, 1046
149.	Clement II, Saxony, Dec. 24, 1046, to Oct. 9, 1047
150.	Benedict IX (third time), Nov. 8, 1047, to July 17, 1048
151.	Damasus II, Bavaria, July 17, 1048, to Aug. 9, 1048
152.	St. Leo IX, Alsace, Feb. 12, 1049, to Apr. 19, 1054
153.	Victor II, Swabia, Apr. 16, 1055, to July 28, 1057
154.	Stephen IX, Lorraine, Aug. 3, 1057, to Mar. 29, 1058
155.	Nicholas II, Burgundy, Jan. 24, 1059, to July 27, 1061
156.	Alexander II, Milan, Oct. 1, 1061, to Apr. 21, 1073
157.	St. Gregory VII, Tuscany, Apr. 22, 1073, to May 25, 1085
158.	Blessed Victor III, Benevento, May 24, 1086, to Sept. 16, 1087
159.	Blessed Urban II, France, Mar. 12, 1088, to July 29, 1099
160.	Paschal II, Ravenna, Aug. 13, 1099, to Jan. 21, 1118
161.	Gelasius II, Gaeta, Jan. 24, 1118, to Jan. 28, 1119
162.	Callistus II, Burgundy, Feb. 2, 1119, to Dec. 13, 1124
163.	Honorius II, Imola, Dec. 15, 1124, to Feb. 13, 1130
164.	Innocent II, Rome, Feb. 14, 1130, to Sept. 24, 1143
165.	Celestine II, Citta di Castello, Sept. 26, 1143, to Mar. 8, 1144
166.	Lucius II, Bologna, Mar. 12, 1144, to Feb. 15, 1145
167.	Blessed Eugene III, Pisa, Feb. 15, 1145, to July 8, 1153
168.	Anastasius IV, Rome, July 12, 1153, to Dec. 3, 1154
169.	Adrian VI, England, Dec. 4, 1154, to Sept. 1, 1159
170.	Alexander III, Siena, Sept. 7, 1159, to Aug. 30 1181

171. Lucius III, Lucca, Sept. 1, 1181, to Sept. 25, 1185
172. Urban III, Milan, Nov.25, 1185, to Oct. 20, 1187
173. Gregory VIII, Benevento, Oct. 21, 1187, to Dec. 17, 1187
174. Clement III, Rome, Dec. 19, 1187, to Mar. 1191
175. Celestine III, Rome, Mar. 30, 1191, to Jan 8, 1198
176. Innocent III, Anagni, Jan. 8, 1198, to July 16, 1216
177. Honorius III, Rome, July 18, 1216, to Mar. 18, 1227
178. Gregory IX, Anagni, Mar. 19, 1227, to Aug 22, 1241
179. Celestine IV, Milan, Oct. 25, 1241, to Nov. 10, 1241
180. Innocent IV, Genoa, June 25, 1243, to Dec. 7, 1254
181. Alexander IV, Anagni, Dec. 12, 1254, to May 25, 1261
182. Urban IV, Troyes, Aug. 29, 1261, to Oct. 2, 1264
183. Clement IV, France, Feb. 5, 1265, to Nov. 29, 1268
184. Blessed Gregory X, Piacenza, Sept. 1, 1271, to Jan . 10, 1276
185. Blessed Innocent V, Savoy, Jan. 21, 1276, to June 22, 1276
186. Adrian V, Genoa, July 11, 1276, to Aug. 18, 1276
187. John XXI, Portugal, Sept. 8, 1276, to May 20, 1277
188. Nicholas III, Rome, Nov. 25, 1277, to Aug. 22, 1280
189. Martin IV, France, Feb. 22, 1281, to Mar. 28, 1285
190. Honorious IV, Rome, Apr. 2, 1285, to Apr. 3, 1287
191. Nicholas IV, Ascoli, Feb. 22, 1288, to Apr. 4, 1292
192. St. Celestine V, Isneria, July 5, 1294, to Dec. 13, 1294
193. Boniface VIII, Anagni, Dec. 24, 1294, to Oct. 11, 1303
194. Blessed Benedictt XI, Trevisio, Oct. 22, 1303, to July 7, 1304
195. Clement V, France, June 5, 1305, to Apr. 20, 1314
196. John XXII, Cahors, Aug. 7, 1316, to Dec. 4, 1334
197. Benedict XII, France, Dec. 20, 1334, to Apr. 25, 1342
198. Clement VI, France, Dec. 18, 1342, to Dec. 6, 1352
199. Innocent VI, France, Dec. 18, 1352, to Sept. 12, 1362
200. Blessed Urban V, France, Sept. 28, 1362, to Dec. 19, 1370
201. Gregory XI, France, Dec. 30, 1370, to Mar. 26, 1378
202. Urban VI, Naples, Apr. 8, 1378, to Oct. 15, 1389
203. Boniface IX, Naples, Nov. 2, 1389, to 1404
204. Innocent VII, Sulmona, Oct. 17, 1404, to Nov. 6, 1406
205. Gregory XII, Venice, Nov. 30, 1406, to July 4, 1415
206. Martin V, Rome, Nov. 11, 1417, to Feb. 20, 1431
207. Eugene IV, Venice, Mar. 3, 1431, to Feb. 23, 1447
208. Nicholas V, Sarzana, Mar. 6, 1447, to Mar. 24, 1455
209. Callistus III, Jativa, Apr. 8, 1455, to Aug. 6, 1458
210. Pius II, Siena, Aug. 19, 1458, to Aug. 15, 1464

211. Paul II, Venice, Aug. 30, 1464, to July 26, 1471
212. Sixtus IV, Savona, Aug. 9, 1471, to Aug. 12, 1484
213. Innocent VIII, Genoa, Aug. 29, 1484, to July 25, 1492
214. Alexander VI, Valencia, Aug. 11, 1492, to Aug. 18, 1503
215. Pius III, Siena, Sept. 22, 1503, to Oct. 18, 1503
216. Julius II, Savona, Oct. 31. 1503, to Feb. 21, 1513
217. Leo X, Florence, Mar. 9, 1513, to Dec. 1, 1521
218. Adrian VI, Utrecht, Jan. 9, 1522, to Sept. 14, 1523
219. Clement VII, Florence, Nov. 19, 1523, to Sept. 25, 1534
220. Paul III, Rome, Feb. 7, 1535, to Mar. 23, 1549
221. Julius III, Rome, Oct. 13, 1550, to Nov. 10, 1554
222. Marcellus II, Montepulciano, Jan. 5, 1555, to May 1, 1555
223. Paul IV, Naples, May 23, 1555, to Aug. 18, 1559
224. Pius IV, Milan, Dec. 25, 1559, to Dec. 9, 1565
225. St. Pius V, Alexandria, Jan. 7, 1566 to May 1, 1572
226. Gregory XIII, Bologna, May 13, 1572, to Apr. 10, 1585
227, Sixtus V, Ripatransone, Apr. 24, 1585, to Aug. 27. 1590
228. Urban VII, Rome, Sept. 15, 1590, to Sept. 27, 1590
229. Gregory XIV, Cremona, Dec. 5, 1590, to Oct. 16, 1591
230. Innocent IX, Bologna, Oct. 29, 1591, to Dec. 30, 1591
231. Clement VIII, Florence, Jan. 30, 1592, to Mar. 3, 1605
232. Leo XI, Florence, Apr. 1, 1605, to Apr. 27, 1605
233. Paul V, Rome, May 16, 1605, to Jan. 28, 1621
234. Gregory XV, Bologna, Feb. 9, 1621, to July 8, 1623
235. Urban VIII, Florence, Aug. 6, 1623, to July 29, 1644
236. Innocent X, Florence, Sept. 15, 1644, to Jan. 7. 1655
237. Alexander VII, Siena, Apr. 7, 1655, to May 22, 1667
238. Clement IX, Pistoia, June 20, 1667, to Dec. 9, 1669
239. Clement X, Rome, Apr. 29, 1670, to July 22, 1676
240. Blessed Innocent XI, Como, Sept. 21, 1676, to Aug. 12, 1689
241. Alexander VIII, Venice, Oct. 6, 1689, to Feb. 1, 1691
242. Innocent XII, Spinazzola, July 12, 1691, to Sept. 27, 1700
243. Clement XI, Urbino, Nov. 23, 1700, to Mar. 19, 1721
244. Innocent XIII, Rome, May 8, 1721, to Mar. 7, 1724
245. Benedict XIII, Gravina, May 29, 1724, to Feb. 21, 1730
246. Clement XII, Florence, July 12, 1730, to Feb. 6, 1740
247. Benedict XIV, Bologna, Aug. 17, 1740, to May 3, 1758
248. Clement XIII, Venice, July 6, 1758, to Feb 2, 1769
249. Clement XIV, Rimini, May 19, 1769, to Sept. 22, 1774
250. Pius VI, Cesena, Feb. 15, 1775, to Aug. 29, 1799

251. Pius VII, Cesena, Mar. 14, 1800, to Aug. 20, 1823
252. Leo XII, Genga, Sept. 28, 1823, to Feb. 10, 1829
253. Pius VIII, Cingoli, Mar. 31, 1829, to Nov. 30, 1830
254. Gregory XVI, Belluno, Feb. 2, 1831, to June 1, 1846
255. Pius IX, Senigallia, June 16, 1846, to Feb. 7, 1878
256. Leo XIII, Carpineto, Feb. 20, 1878 to Aug. 20, 1903
257. St. Pius X, Riese, Aug. 4, 1903, to Aug. 20, 1914
258. Benedict XV, Genoa, Sept. 3, 1914, to Jan. 22, 1922
259. Pius XI, Milan, Feb 6, 1922, to Feb. 10, 1939
260. Pius XII, Rome, Mar. 2, 1939, to Oct. 9, 1958
261. John XXIII, Bergamo, Oct. 28, 1958, to June 3, 1963
262. Paul VI, Brescia, June 21, 1963, to Aug. 6, 1978
263. John Paul I, Canale d' Agordo, Aug. 26, 1978, to Sept. 28, 1978
264. John Paul II, Poland, Oct. 16, 1978 to ――――

THE TESTIMONY OF 2000 YEARS

If the testimony of 2000 years does not effectively prove the Church of Rome to be the Institution founded by Jesus Christ on the Rock of Peter, **then the world has no Church of Christ at all!**

Through 2,000 years, amidst the widest possible variety of circumstances, the teachings of the Catholic Church have never swerved from the highest moral standard. On occasions – as in the case of King Henry VIII – the Church has preferred to lose everything rather than compromise in regard to the high morality of her doctrines. Rather than grant Henry the VIII his request, the Church preferred to lose the entire country of England!

A non-Catholic, O. Pfleiderer said "In spite of all Protestant attempts to weaken its force, it cannot be doubted that this passage (Mt 16:18) contains the solemn proclamation of the primacy of Peter. He is declared to be the foundation of the Church, the bearer of the keys and the sovereign lawgiver, whose precepts and prohibitions have the force of divinely sanctioned laws" (*Fundamental Theology,* page 119, Herder, St. Louis, 1931).

With the multiplicity of religious beliefs in the world today, there is an error that says: "It does not matter to which of the denominations you belong – Anglican, Baptist, Methodist, Lutheran, etc. – for Christ founded but one Church, a spiritual body with no earthly organization, and of that Church one only has to be Baptized and accept the Lord Jesus Christ as your savior."

Contrary to the above, in the Gospels we see Christ setting up a visible organization, with a central authority and properly constituted officials, each with definite functions to perform regarding the Church as The Mystical Body of Christ which can be approached by, and which can excommunicate, its

65

members: "If he will not hear them, tell the Church, and if he will not hear theChurch, let him be to thee as the heathen and publican" (Mt 18:17). His words, "tell the Church," would be impossible of fulfillment if the Church were merely a spiritual society, which so many today believe.

"Where Peter is, there is the Church," said St. Ambrose. "According to the promise of the Lord," said St. Thomas Aquinas, "the apostolic Church of St. Peter and its Pontiffs, and in the full faith and authority of Peter remains free from all taint of heresy and deceit. And while other churches are shamed by errors, she reigns the solitary Church unshakably established, imposing silence and closing the mouths of heretics. And we, of necessity for our salvation, must proclaim and profess this pattern of holy, apostolic tradition."

St. Frances Xavier Cabrini said, "Who is the Holy Father? He is the representative of God, of His authority and majesty among men. The Holy Father is the instrument of the Holy Ghost, the depository of the treasures and secrets of God. He is the key of knowledge for the Christian people. He has inhis keeping the power to loose and to bind. The voice of the Holy Father is the voice of God. His word is the word of God. He is the living ark of the New Testament in which is contained the purity of the Catholic faith. The Pope must be considered the guide of the people and the ark of salvation for everyone."

St. Robert Bellarmine, who lived in the wake of the principal Protestant reformers (1542-1621), not only said, "The one and true Church is the assembly of men, bound together by the profession of the same Christian faith, and by the communion of the same sacraments, under the rule of legitimate pastors, and in particular of the one Vicar of Christ on earth, the Roman Pontiff," but he expanded on the Four Marks of the true Church by listing 15:

1. Name: Catholic; worldwide and not confined to a particular nation;
2. Antiquity, in tracing ancestry directly to Christ;
3. Duration, lasting substantially unchanged for centuries;
4. Extensiveness, in the number of members [there are 1 billion today!];
5. Episcopal succession, from the twelve Apostles to the current hierarchy;
6. Doctrinal agreement between current teaching and Apostolic Church;
7. Union among members, and between members and visible head (Pope);
8. Holiness of doctrine, reflecting the holiness of God;
9. Efficacy of doctrine, reflecting the holiness of God;
10. Holiness of life of representative writers and defenders;
11. Miracles worked in the Church and under its auspices;
12. Prophecy gift among its saints and spokespersons;
13. Opposition aroused on same ground as Christ was opposed;

14. Unhappy end of her enemies;

15. Temporal peace and earthly happiness of those who are faithful to her teaching and defend her interests.

THEY CANNOT HARM HER

Considered the most accurate account of the lives of the popes is the collected writings of Ludwig von Pastor, a German historian, to whom Pope Leo XIII gave permission to examine in every detail in the Vatican archives. In speaking about the most notorious of the "bad popes," Pope Alexander VI, van Pastor says quite clearly:

"Alexander never did anything that justly deserves blame in matters concerning the Church. Even his bitterest enemies are unable to formulate any accusations against him in this respect. Her doctrines, the Church's doctrines, were maintained in all their purity (The gates of hell, even when the papacy is held by an unworthy incumbent, do not prevail against the Church in correspondence to Christ's precious promise).

"It seemed as though Alexander's reign was meant by Providence to demonstrate the truth that although men may hurt the Church, they **cannot harm her.** In the Church there have always been unworthy priests as well as bad Christians, and that no one might be scandalized by this, Our Lord Himself foretold it. He likens the Church to a field in which the weeds grow up with the wheat, or to a net in which both good and bad fish are caught. Even among His own disciples, He endured a Judas Iscariot.

"Just as the intrinsic worth of a jewel is not lessened by an inferior setting, so the sins of a priest cannot essentially affect his power of offering the Holy Sacrifice, or administering the Sacraments . . . The personal holiness of the priest is of the highest importance for the lives of the faithful, inasmuch as he constitutes a living example for them to follow and compels the respect and esteem of those who are outside the Church. Still, the goodness or the badness of the minister can exercise no substantial influence on the being, the divine character or the holiness of the Church, on the word of revelation, on the graces and spiritual powers with which she is endowed. Thus, even the Supreme High Priest can in no way diminish the value of that heavenly treasure which he controls and dispenses, but only as a steward.

"The gold remains gold in impure as well as in pure hands. The papal office belongs to a higher sphere than the personality of its occupant for the time being, and can neither gain nor lose in its essential dignity by his saintliness on the one side or his unworthiness on the other. Even the first Pope, St. Peter, had sinned before he was given this commission in denying his Lord and Master, and yet the office of the Supreme Pastor was given to him."

CHAPTER EIGHT—THE FOUNTAIN OF IMMORTAL GRACE

St. Peter tells us that, by God's life, we have become sharers in the "divine nature" (2 Pt 1:4). In other words, while remaining human beings, we actually share, when we are in the state of grace, in the very life of God Himself.

The *Catechism of the Catholic Church* sums up the doctrine of grace by saying, "Grace is *favor*, the *free and undeserved help* that God gives us to respond to his call to become children of God, adoptive sons, partakers of the divine nature and eternal life. Grace is a *participation in the life of God*. It introduces us into the intimacy of Trinitarian life." The very last words of the Bible are: "The grace of Our Lord Jesus Christ be with all. Amen."

The Mass brings us more grace than anything else we can possibly do. Vatican 11 tells us: "from the Eucharist, grace is poured forth upon us as from a fountain, and the sanctification of men in Christ and the glorification of God to which all other activities of the Church are directed, as toward their end, are achieved with maximum effectiveness."

"The real Presence of Christ in the Eucharist," said Fr. T. A. Johnson, S.J., "is one of the most mysterious doctrines of the Catholic Faith, yet it is the center and explanation of the whole Catholic system. The whole life of the Church revolves around the Blessed Sacrament. And surely it must be so, since the Eucharist means that the Man, Jesus Christ, God in His Human Presence, is still in the world, present with us to comfort and strengthen us."

"When Jesus ascended into Heaven," he continues, "His Visible Bodily Presence was removed from earth, and as Man He would have ceased altogether to be present with us were it not that He devised a method whereby He might still be with us, though not in outward visible form. The Blessed Sacrament secures that God is permanently on earth in His Human Nature and with His Human Presence."

The Eucharist is spiritual nourishment for the spiritual life. It does all for the life of the soul that ordinary food does for the body. It repairs loss of spiritual vitality. It promotes progress towards a perfect development in holiness. And it gives the joy of health in the spiritual order. It sustains the life of grace and grace is the indispensable means necessary to reach heaven; it makes us holy and grants us a participation in the divine life. As the rational soul is the principle of a human being's natural life, sanctifying grace is the vital principle of the supernatural life. It is often associated with the virtue of charity however it is different in that charity belongs to the will, whereas sanctifying grace belongs to the whole soul, mind, will and affections.

There is one essential difference, of course, between the activity of the Eucharist, and that of ordinary food. Ordinary food nourishes our bodies by becoming absorbed and transformed into our own living tissues and cells. But the opposite process occurs in the Eucharist. Holy Communion absorbs us into a unity with Christ. It is a greater and stronger food than any merely natural food. Instead of merely fostering our natural life, it intensifies our participation in a higher, supernatural life of grace.

The greatest of all errors is to live each day without being in the state of grace. A renowned German theologian of the 19th century, Fr. Matthias J. Scheeben, tells us to "endeavor to become more and more like Christ, your Heavenly Model. Be not guided by the laws of a perverted world, but by the law of grace and of the Holy Spirit. By constant striving after every virtue, keep yourself on the lofty height to which grace has raised you. Soar above the earth and above your own nature through intimate communion with God, your Father. Keep yourself, as much as possible, through constant prayer, in the vestibule of Heaven. This [type of] life alone offers an occupation worthy of your high dignity; in it alone is the realization of the supernatural, divine life that the children of God should lead."

HOW TO KNOW YOU ARE IN THE STATE OF GRACE

Four Doctors of the Church furnish us with their inspired writings to determine if we are living in the state of grace:

1) St. Alphonsus Liguori: "The Resolution to make every effort and to die rather than commit any deliberate sin, however small, frees us from every obstacle to moving ahead; and, at the same time, gives us great courage because it assures us that we are in God's grace."

2) St. Francis de Sales: "The best guarantee we can have, in this world, of being in the grace of God is not the feelings that we have of his love, but the pure and irrevocable abandonment of our whole being into his hands and in the firm resolve never to consent to any sin, either great or small."

3) St. Thomas Aquinas: "The common signs that we are in the state of grace: "Keeping the Commandments for a long time, devotion to Christ and to His Blessed Mother, hatred of sin, contempt for worldly things, and peace of soul. Anyone who finds these signs in his life can be morally certain that he possesses the grace of God and, if he perseveres, will enter into eternal life."

4) St. Augustine: "Do you wish to ascertain whether you live in the state of grace, whether you enjoy friendship with God, whether you are a real disciple of Christ, whether you live according to His Spirit? Ask yourself if you love your neighbor, if you love him for the sake of God? The answer to the latter question will also be an infallible one to the former."

MEDICINE OF IMMORTALITY

St. Cyril of Alexandria, Father and Doctor of the Church, wrote: "If the poison of pride is swelling up in you, turn to the Eucharist; and that Bread, Which is your God humbling and disguising Himself, will teach you humility. If the fever of selfish greed rages in you, feed on this Bread; and you will learn generosity. If the cold wind of coveting withers you, hasten to the Bread of Angels; and charity will come to blossom in your heart. If you feel the itch of intemperance, nourish yourself with the Flesh and Blood of Christ, Who practiced heroic self-control during His earthly life; and you will become temperate. If you are lazy and sluggish about spiritual things, strengthen yourself with this heavenly Food; and you will grow fervent. Lastly, if you feel scorched by the fever of impurity, go to the banquet of the Angels; and the spotless Flesh of Christ will make you pure and chaste."

AGE OF UNBELIEF

Modern man has made himself the absolute center of reality, having himself falsely occupy the place of God. He wants to believe there is no God – then right and wrong are merely opinions, and man has license to sin.

He forgets that it is not man who made God, but God who made man. Apart from Jesus, we do not know what God, life, death or we ourselves really are. It is not surprising that a culture without God ends in a culture without hope, because only in God, who is eternal love, does the heart of man finds its origin and its true end.

John Lennon of the Beatles had been raised a Christian and attended Sunday school at St. Peter's Church in Liverpool, England. Reference to Christianity can be found in some of his lyrics.

In 1966, reporter Maureen Cleave, a friend of John Lennon's, published an article about him in the London Evening Standard. The article contained various quotes from a recent conversation she had with him, including Lennon's view of the current state of religion. He said: "Christianity will go. It will vanish and shrink. I needn't argue about that. I am right and I will be proved right. We're more popular than Jesus now."

The last sentence of that quote became a headline in the U.S. papers and caused an enormous reaction. In subsequent interviews Lennon apologized for what he said and explained that by saying that the Beatles were more popular than Jesus, he was not bragging but simply stating a fact, and raising questions about the state of religion.

Little do those who turn away from God realize that the very power that allows them to exist demands faith. T.A. Johnston, S.J., said:

"The Sacred Host . . . hidden in the Tabernacle . . . is the very Foundation of the Force that made and preserves the world; that there is life – the Life! But there it is. Anyone who gets into vital contact with God truly present in the Blessed Sacrament – and that is what a true visit to the Blessed Sacrament so much facilitates – can do more in one second, than by means of all the merely human activity imaginable.

"People totally wrapped up in the material goods of the world cannot comprehend what pleasure can be found in spending time before the Tabernacle; but to souls who love God, hours passed before the Blessed Sacrament seem as moments because of the celestial sweetness the Lord gives them to taste and enjoy."

FAITH SEES THE INVISIBLE

Jesus spoke these words to St. Margaret Mary Alacoque: "I have a burning thirst to be honored by men in the Blessed Sacrament"; and, to the Apostles "Could you not watch one hour with me?" (Mt 26:40).

All through the ages He has demanded this same Faith of His followers. It is by means of this light of Faith that we are able to see Him under the veils of the Holy Eucharist. We genuflect, we bow deeply. We repeat the words of "doubting Thomas" when he was overwhelmed with belief: "My Lord and my God!" Of course, we adore Christ on the altar, in the tabernacle, in the monstrance at benediction, and in procession. This is, above all, the Sacrament of love. The senses cannot see Christ in the Eucharist. We see Him only by Faith. As St. Cyril reminds us, "Do not doubt whether this is true. Since He is truth, He cannot lie." He is the way, the truth, and the life.

FEAST OF CORPUS CHRISTI

Throughout the world, in June, Catholics celebrate the Feast of Corpus Christi (the Body of Christ). Pope John Paul II requested this Feast be celebrated in Rome with a solemn Eucharistic Procession after Mass. The Blessed Sacrament is taken to four outdoor altars, each representing one of the Gospel writers. At each altar the Gospel proclaiming the institution of the Holy Eucharist is proclaimed and Benediction given.

The feast of Corpus Christi originated in 1264 when Pope Urban IV instituted the feast day "to compensate for the lack of reverence exhibited daily at the celebration of the Holy Mass and for transgressions committed through negligence."

All the Masses we attend celebrate the real presence of Jesus under the form of bread and wine; however, on the Feast of Corpus Christi special attention is given to this sacred mystery in a very solemn manner.

72

In Poland it is customary to hold great processions through the streets of every city for eight days in honor of this mystery. It is an amazing testimony to the faith of the Polish people to see the main streets of Warsaw, Krakow, Lowic, Poznan, etc. filled with a human sea moving with the Blessed Sacrament to a number of flower bedecked shrines set in every major square. The same scene of faith is repeated in every city, town and village.

Parishioners spend days preparing the various shrines where Our Lord, in the Blessed Eucharist, will come for a few minutes. Each altar is a magnificent work of art whose only purpose is to welcome Our Savior for a few brief minutes.

Little girls are given the privilege of dressing in white and of scattering flowers and petals before the priest carrying the Holy Sacrament. For the boys, small Corpus Christi Bells are provided to be rung as they follow Our Eucharistic Lord. Every religious, social and civic organization, takes part carrying banners, icons, flowers, candles and flags, leading the Eucharist, from shrine to shrine. The city streets, just for a day, are transformed into a vast cathedral.

In America, Polish Americans continue to honor Our Lord in the Most Holy Sacrament with processions around their churches and with beautifully decorated altars.

Like Pope Urban, Pope John Paul II also wanted to increase devotion to the Blessed Sacrament. His goal was threefold:

1. He wished an increase of devotion to the Blessed Sacrament.

2. He wanted Catholics to visit the Blessed Sacrament more frequently in their parish churches.

3. He wanted the faithful to receive Our Blessed Lord in the Holy Eucharist more frequently.

FAITH IN THE REAL PRESENCE

When Saul of Tarsus was traveling the road to Damascus on his mission of persecuting Christians, he was suddenly stricken from his horse. A blinding light shone upon him, while he heard a voice saying, "Saul, Saul, why do you persecute me?" Dazzled and amazed, Saul asked, "Who are you Lord?" "I am Jesus," replied the voice, "whom you are persecuting."

A miracle of grace transformed the persecutor Saul into the great Apostle Paul. "This man," said the Lord, "is to me a vessel of election, to carry my name before the Gentiles, and kings, and the children of Israel." He was to become the champion convert-maker of all time, the everlasting symbol of the mysterious power of God's grace.

What happened to Saul has happened in different ways to individuals in succeeding centuries. God's grace strikes like a bolt of lightning. From scoffing skeptics they are changed into ardent believers and zealous apostles. One who experienced that transforming miracle of grace is Alma Grayce Miller.

"I was born and reared in Meadville, Pennsylvania," she said, "but lived in Washington D.C., for the past seventeen years, where I have a studio and teach piano and organ. I come to Meadville every summer to visit friends and relatives.

"We were strict Methodists, and I was organist in the Stone Methodist Church here for a long time. I was prejudiced against the Catholic Church and had little to do with Catholics. There was only one Catholic family in Meadville, Mr. and Mrs. Ralph Shadley, with whom I became acquainted and whose friendship I cherished.

THE BLESSED SACRAMENT IS IMPELLING

"The Shadleys had a young son, Fritzie, who attended St. Agatha's grade school. When he was about ten he became an altar boy. One day he called on me. 'Miss Miller,' he said, 'we are going to have Forty Hours Devotion next Sunday, and I would like to have you come and see me march in procession.'

"I thought so much of Fritzie that I hated to disappoint him. So I told him I'd be there to see him march if I could get someone to take my place at the Methodist church. I managed it.

"I had never been in a Catholic Church before. I took a seat in the middle aisle under the choir loft. I sat in the pew but would not get on my knees. The pastor, Fr. Andrew Weschler, noted for his zeal in winning converts, sang the Mass and opened the Forty Hours. I scoffed at the whole procedure and wondered how stupid Catholics must be to believe that Our Lord is really present in the consecrated Host.

"After Mass the procession came slowly down the middle aisle. In the long line of altar boys was little Fritzie, carrying a lighted candle and looking like an angel. Nearer and nearer came the celebrant carrying the Blessed Sacrament. All around me people were on their knees, bowing their heads in adoration as the celebrant reached their pews. I would not get down on my knees; I said to myself, I'd sit tight.

"But when the Blessed Sacrament reached my pew, I fell down on my knees, moved as by a force I couldn't resist. 'This is no phony,' I found myself saying. 'This is the real thing; I am in the presence of God Himself!' I was moved as I had never been before, and my heart was strangely warmed. Tears came unbidden to my eyes. I went back to Washington, took instructions, was baptized and received into the Church. The next day when I received Our Lord in Holy Communion was the happiest in my life.

"At first I couldn't understand that strange commotion which came over me at St. Agatha's. But I know now. It was the grace of God streaming to me from the Blessed Sacrament. It brought me weeping to my knees and it came to me through that innocent little child who invited me."

HOMAGE TO THE BLESSED SACRAMENT

George Guynemer was France's greatest loved pilot of Word War I. He was a brilliant aviator whose country called him "The bright sword of France." When he was asked where he obtained his courage, he pointed to the Tabernacle. He went to Mass and Holy Communion daily plus making visits to the Blessed Sacrament whenever the opportunity presented itself. Admired by everyone, when he was missing in action, it was said of him: "He flew so high that he never came down – he flew to his God."

In the same World War, another great pilot, Captain Albert Ball of England, was also a hero. Stationed in France, his base was located near a Catholic Church. As he flew by the Church, to and from his battles, he always made it a point to dip the wings of his aircraft as a symbol of homage to Jesus Christ present in the Blessed Sacrament.

SLAVE AND SAINT

Pierre Toussaint was born in Haiti in 1766. He moved to New York with his owner and died "in the odor of sanctity," on June 30, 1853. The Archbishop of New York started the process of his beatification. Pope John Paul II has declared Pierre Toussaint 'venerable' making the Haitian–born American slave one step closer to sainthood. Toussaint will become the first black U.S. saint when canonized.

Toussaint was born in 1766 in Santo Domingo on the sugar plantation owned by Jean Berard. According to biographer Ellen Tarry, the author of *The Other Toussaint,* he was a fortunate slave. The French Black Code of 1685, promulgated by Louis XIV, demanded that slaves be baptized, given religion instruction, and rest on Sundays and feast days. Pierre's grandmother and parents were the favorite slaves of the Berard family, French Catholics of high status. The Toussaints were responsible both for the plantations and for collecting the harvest.

When one of the Berard son's moved to New York with his wife Marie, he took Pierre with him and had him train as a barber. His skills, inventiveness, humility and honesty were well known in the city. His charity was outstanding. When the young Jean Berard's fortune dwindled to nothing, he returned to Santo

Domingo where he died of pleurisy while his wife remained in New York. Almost penniless, Toussaint supported Marie Berard for almost 20 years until she died, without ever asking anything in return, out of respect and charity for the family.

Marie Berard freed Toussaint before her death. Now, able to support a family of his own, he married Juliette Noel, the love of his life. He was 45 when he married. His biographer does not mention any children born to the couple.

The Toussaints became famous throughout the city for giving food and shelter to many homeless children. Their charity in assisting immigrants and other people in need, both Catholics and Protestants, was unlimited and heroic. Pierre and Juliette needed much inner strength to carry on the many charitable activities they were involved in. They found it in the reception of the Holy Eucharist, and in prayer before the Blessed Sacrament in the original St. Patrick's Cathedral.

The name of Pierre Toussaint doesn't appear in history books, but Cardinal John O'Connor of New York firmly believed in Pierre Toussaint. Toussaint's body was transferred recently from the cemetery of the old St. Patrick Cathedral to the crypt under the main altar of St. Patrick's Cathedral on Fifth Avenue, reserved for the hierarchical authorities of New York. To no other layman has such an honor ever been given. He now rests alongside of such illustrious persons as Archbishop Fulton J. Sheen, Cardinal Patrick Hayes, Cardinal Francis Spellman, Cardinal Terence Cook, and Cardinal John O'Connor.

SAINT PADRE PIO

Born Francis Forgione on May 25, 1887, Padre Pio was gifted with extraordinary graces; he shined like a light. Radiant in virtue he performed edifying actions that mirrored Christ and encouraged the faithful to greater efforts toward sanctity. The reason for these gifts is to spread the Kingdom of God by rescuing sinners from the grip of Satan and by restoring all things in Christ.

Padre Pio is the first priest to receive the stigmata of Christ in the 2000 year history of the Church, and one of a handful of saints who was given the gifts of heavenly fragrance, bi-location, reading hearts, miracles, levitation, and prophecy. Padre Pio accomplished many miraculous cures – testified by thousands of witnesses – throughout the world. His humility was such that he would remark: "I performed no miracle! It was God who cured you! Thank Him; don't thank me!"

Many people who came near his stigmatized hands or his clothing, or any objects touched by him, noticed a sweet perfume. Sometimes this perfume could be smelled at great distances, such as in America, Asia, and Africa. The odor was of roses, violets, or lilies; at times of tobacco or incense. Its meaning

76

revealed the presence of Padre Pio, even if he could not be seen. It was often proof that he had heard or was responding to a prayer.

He had an extraordinary influence on many souls. People merely had to see him to be moved to approach him and open up their consciences to him. He counseled all that came to him, and they came in droves. He heard confessions practically all of his waking hours – up to 18 hours a day! Atheists, fallen-away Catholics, unbelievers, and Protestants were converted by being in his presence.

Frederick Abresch, a convert from Protestantism, was so impressed by Padre Pio that he took up residence in San Giovanni Rotundo to be near the saintly priest each day of his life. His wife bore him a son and Padre Pio prophesied that he would be a priest someday. Today he is a priest working in the Vatican – he is Msgr. Pio Abresch named after Padre Pio.

Padre Pio ascribed the success of his priestly life to Mary, the Mother of all graces, and to her powerful intercession. From his youth he always had a tender and childlike love for Mary. He was consecrated to her; she held a special place in his life and prayers. He said rosary after rosary each day; the rosary was seldom, if ever, seen out of his hands. His whole life was Jesus and Mary. Because they had been together in life, they had to be treated together in his prayers. As Mary had been God's instrument to bring Christ into the world, so she also would bring all mankind back to Christ.

Padre Pio died on September 23, 1968. He was mourned all over the world. It is estimated that 100,000 people from all parts of the world attended his funeral. On May 2, 1999, Padre Pio was beatified by Pope John Paul II and on June 16, 2002, in the presence of 300,000 people, he was canonized St. Pio of Pietrelcina. This was the most popular and largest gathering of people for a canonization ever. His exemplary charity for souls can be summed up in his own words – "I can refuse no one. How can I when the Lord never refuses me a grace!"

Padre Pio claimed that those who thought they could go through life without the help of our Blessed Lady were foolish. He said "I wish I had a voice strong enough to invite sinners of the world to love Our Lady. But since this is not within my power, I have prayed and will pray to my dear angel to perform this task for me." One of his tributes to Our Blessed Lady was "May Mary fill your heart with the flowers and fragrances of ever-fresh virtues, and place her maternal hand on your head. Always keep close to our Heavenly Mother, because she is the sea that must be crossed, in order to reach the shores of eternal splendor in the kingdom of dawn."

When Padre Pio was asked if Our Lady had been present at Mass, he replied: "Yes, she placed herself to the side, but I could see her; what joy! What paradise!" "Has she attended only once, or is she always present?" Padre Pio

77

answered, "How can the mother of Jesus, present at Calvary at the foot of the cross, who offered her Son as victim for the salvation of souls, be absent at the mystical Calvary of the altar?" "Is Our Lady present at all Masses that are being celebrated in the world?" Padre Pio replied, "Yes."

Of the Mass which gives us the Holy Eucharist, the fountain of immortal grace, Padre Pio said, "We could sooner live with out the sun than we could the Mass." And, of Adoration, he proclaimed: "A thousand years of enjoying human glory is not worth even an hour spent sweetly communing with Jesus in the Blessed Sacrament."

And of the Rosary, when his Superior had asked him how many rosaries he had said that day, he answered: "Well, to my Superior I must tell the truth, I have said thirty-four today." It is no wonder Pio was called "the living Rosary." He was known to recite as many as forty rosaries in one day. His advice always to all is to hold the weapon of Mary tight in your hand. It will bring you victory over your enemies.

The day Padre Pio died, he held his Rosary in his hand for the last time. With his dying breath he uttered his last two favorite words: "Jesus and Mary."

CHAPTER NINE—THE INDISPENSABLE CONDITION

Faith is the greatest demand that can be made of a soul – it is the spiritual life! Jesus said: "Everything is possible to one who has faith" (Mk 9:22). Jesus never says "By my power you have been cured, or by my power you have been saved." It is your faith in His infinite power which is the indispensable condition that is required.

Before Jesus performed a miracle, He always asked for an act of faith. "Do you believe that I can do this?" (Mt 9:28); and when faith was sincere, the miracle took place immediately! "Courage daughter, your faith has saved you" (Mt 9:22), He said to the woman who was troubled with an issue of blood. And the woman was cured. To the Canaanite Mother: "Woman, great is thy Faith, be it done unto thee as thou wilt." To the woman who touched His garment: "Daughter, thy Faith has made thee whole." To the blind Bartimeus: "Go thy way, thy Faith has made thee whole." To the Centurion seeking a cure for his servant: "Amen, I say to you, I have not found so great Faith in Israel . . . Go and as thou hast believed so be it done to thee."

St. Matthew records ten different occasions where Jesus cured every one of the great numbers of sick people brought to him:

1) "He went around all of Galilee . . . curing every disease among the people" (Mt 4:23).

2) "His fame spread to all of Syria, and they brought to Him all who were sick with various diseases and racked with pain, those who were possessed, lunatics, and paralytics, and He cured them" (Mt 4:24). [Notice, they brought "all" who were sick, not just selected cases, and He "cured them" all.]

3) "And, when crowds brought great numbers of sick, He cured them. He cured all the sick" (Mt 8:16).

4) "He cured every disease and illness" (Mt 9:35).

5) "He cured them all" (Mt 12:15).

6) "He saw the vast crowd . . . and cured their sick" (Mt 14:14).

7) "And as many as touched His cloak were healed" (Mt 14:35).

8) "Great crowds came to Him having with them the lame, the blind, the deformed, the mute, and many others. They placed them at His feet and He cured them" (Mt 15:30).

9) "Great crowds followed Him and He cured them there" (Mt 19:2).

10) "The blind and the lame approached Him in the Temple area and He cured them" (Mt 21: 14).

No mortal has ever accomplished anything comparable; no mortal has ever even claimed to be able to do it! Imagine a person sitting by the roadside and seeing crowds of sick people being brought to a neighboring town where Jesus is healing the sick and the incurable. Later he sees the same people, the blind, the lame, people with leprosy, with hideous scars, with physical defects, and deformities of various kinds, all coming back entirely cured. What more proof is needed to verify to the spectator that spectacular miracles have occurred; that this truly is a Divine person – God and man – and not a mere mortal!

FAITH REWARDED

St. John Vianney, with tears in his eyes, would point to the Tabernacle and say "He is there!" St. Peter Julian Eymard also pointed to the Tabernacle, and with joyful fervor exclaimed, "There Jesus is!"

Few people are familiar with the remarkable faith Mrs. Vaughn – the mother of the famous Jesuit preacher, Cardinal Bernard Vaughn, S.J. – had in Our Lord's presence in the Tabernacle.

Despite the responsibility of so many children – thirteen, eight boys and five girls – she made it a point to visit Our Lord in the Tabernacle, daily, to present her requests to Him who said: "Ask and you shall receive."

While she prayed, her daughter, Gladys, who used to accompany her, was amazed at the transformation of her mother's face. "Mother, why do you always look so much prettier when you pray?" Mrs. Vaughn looking towards the Tabernacle smiled and said: "My darling, Jesus is there!" From then on Gladys would keep her eyes on the Tabernacle door and repeat to herself, "Jesus is there."

Mrs. Vaughn spent from five to six each evening with Our Lord, praying that all her children might serve Him in the Convent or the Sanctuary. What an answer she received! Five daughters became nuns, and six of her sons became priests, one, Cardinal-Archbishop of Westminster, England, another Archbishop of Sydney, Australia.

It was God's will that two of her boys should practice and proclaim their Faith as laymen. All were children of prayer.

ABOVE REASON

There have been great geniuses in every century; but they all fade in the presence of Jesus. The crowds followed Him for long days without tiring of hearing Him: "Never did man speak like this man" (Jn 7:46).

He was wisdom personified; He was conscious of it and He proved it in a most striking fashion: "I am the way, the truth and the life" (Jn 14:6); "I am the light of the world. Whoever follows me will not walk in darkness, but will have the light of life" (Jn 8:12). He could boldly exclaim what no man could ever say: "Which of you can convict me of sin?" (Jn 8:46).

He taught an admirable morality which is summed up in the love of God and the love of neighbor. He insists that we love God above all things, even if

80

we must sacrifice our life; He orders us to love all men without exception, even our enemies, to do to them the good that we would have them do to us.

Reason tells us that our religion would not be divine if it were not above reason. God would not be God if He is not incomprehensible, and my soul could not adore Him if my mind could understand Him.

FAITH IN A MAN – FAITH IN A GOD-MAN

The Detroit News carried a phenomenal story in their sports section of December 12, 2000, with the caption: "Alex Rodriguez signed the largest contract in pro sports history, $252 million for 10 years with the Texas Rangers!"

The article continued: "The contract calls for a $10 million signing bonus paid over five years and salaries of $21 million in each of the first four years. He gets $25 million a year in 2005 and 2006, and $27 million in each of the final four seasons.

"The Rangers lured the four-time All-Star shortstop from the Seattle Mariners with a 10 year contract . . . 'Alex is the player we believe will allow this franchise to fulfill its dream of continuing on its path to becoming a World Series champion,' Rangers owner Tom Hicks said."

Alex Rodriguez has faith in a contract, a piece of paper signed in ink by owner Thomas Hicks – a mere mortal man – that tells him he will receive $252 million in 10 years! How much more should we have faith in the Consecrated Bread sealed by the Blood of Jesus Christ – God and Man - that will give us eternal life!

Faith in the Blessed Sacrament is certain because it relies not on the word of man, but on the word of Jesus, the Son of God, who can neither deceive nor be deceived; in this sense we can say that faith is free from errors because no one can doubt God's word. "Not to believe in You, O my God," said St. Mary Magdalen dei Pazzi, "requires more faith than to believe in You. Your love for me is so great that I no longer need faith to believe it."

A recent scholarly poll taken on American college campuses show that eighty-seven percent of non-Latino Catholics, and ninety-five percent of the Latinos, believe that "at Mass, the bread and wine actually become the body and blood of Christ" (*America Magazine,* 3/27/99).

It is belief in the Mass and the Holy Eucharist that bring Catholics to Church on Sunday in such large numbers. A five-year poll, taken from 1996 to 2001, showed that the average Catholic Church in the United States has 1800 people in attendance every Sunday. The poll, which was taken by a non-Catholic organization financed by the Pew Foundation, established that the average non-Catholic church has only from 150 to 300 in attendances on Sunday.

It is the presence of Christ in the form of consecrated bread and wine that makes the difference. As He told the Apostles at the Last Supper, when He distributed His body and blood: "Do this in memory of Me" (Lk 22:19-20).

In the fourth century, St. Cyril of Jerusalem said: "As a life-giving Sacrament we possess the sacred Flesh of Christ and His Precious Blood under the appearance of bread and wine. What seems to be bread is not bread, but Christ's Body: what seems to be wine is not wine, but Christ's Blood."

GOD COULD NOT GIVE MORE

Jesus could not give us a more precious gift than Himself in the Holy Eucharist - His greatest miracle! "The devotion to the Eucharist," said Pope St. Pius X, "is the most noble, because it has God as its object; it is the most profitable for salvation, because it gives us the Author of Grace; it is the sweetest, because the Lord is Sweetness Itself."

In the Holy Eucharist Jesus makes Himself available. He is the food of my soul which must be nourished just as the body needs to be nourished.

Just as ordinary food gives life to our body, Holy Communion gives life to our immortal soul. Thereby we increase the life of grace given to us at Baptism. Holy Communion does so much to keep us from the evil of sin!

In Holy Communion we receive His body, which "is given up for us," and is "shed for many for the forgiveness of sins." The Holy Eucharist helps cleanse us from our past sins, and helps preserve us from sinning in the future.

In writing about this Sacrament, St. Ambrose told us, more than 1600 years ago: "For as often as we eat this bread and drink the cup, we proclaim the death of the Lord, and the forgiveness of sins." As His blood is poured out for the sins of mankind, we should receive Holy Communion often so our sins will be forgiven.

St. Fulgentius urges us, "Let us die to sin and live for God!" In Baptism St. Paul tells us, "We have been called to form but one body . . . who are many are one body, for we all partake of the one bread." In the Eucharist we have the unity of the Mystical Body.

Why are non-Catholic Christians, following the Reformation, separated from the Catholic Church? They have lost the Eucharistic mystery, as they did not keep the Sacrament of Holy Orders, whereby priests have the power to consecrate bread and wine.

The Holy Eucharist is a great mystery, the shining light that lights up every aspect of Catholic life. From it we draw our spiritual life, our strength, our spiritual energy. It is a foretaste of the beatific vision, when we will be with God, face to face.

The Eucharist is the very center and heart of the Mass. The priest prays over the bread and wine. Then, with awe, he consecrates each of them. He elevates the consecrated bread, and then the wine. Through our participation in this great mystery of faith, we share spiritually in Our Lord's passion, death and resurrection. In this way we carry out the command of Christ to celebrate the memorial of His sacrifice, as Christ becomes mysteriously present on the altar.

Honoring and receiving the Holy Eucharist is done in the realization of happiness with God forever. There is no surer pledge or clearer sign of this great hope than receiving Holy Communion, particularly at Mass. It is the one bread that provides the medicine of eternal life. As St. Ignatius of Antioch wrote, more than 1900 years ago: "Every time this mystery is celebrated, the work of our redemption is carried on, as we break the bread that makes us live forever in Jesus Christ."

Pope John Paul II noted, in his beautiful exhortation, *The Church in America:* "The Eucharist is the outstanding moment of encounter with the Living Christ . . . It is the source and summit of the Church's life, an invitation to solidarity as expressed in Our Lord's commandment: 'Love one another as I have loved you.'" (Jn 13:34).

The Holy Father's words greatly encourage us to renew our commitment to thank God for the magnificent, miraculous gift of Christ's presence in the Eucharist. It is a gift of infinite love, sinful though we are.

CHAPTER TEN—EUCHARISTIC EVANGELIZATION

Our Church holds an embarrassment of spiritual riches that can be obtained through prayer before, and adoration of, the Blessed Sacrament. The graces are so abundant that even if we were to draw upon them every minute of the day, we could never exhaust them all.

In his message of June 17, 2001, Pope John Paul II told us: "The Church Community gathers around in adoration of the most precious treasure that Christ the Lord left to us: the Sacrament of the Eucharist. Through that Sacrament God sanctifies hearts, people, communities, nations, and the whole cosmos.

"People need the Eucharist, which is a source of strength for evangelization, in order to change the world, and help the neediest. More than ever before, Christians need the Eucharist to promote the 'missionary renewal' . . . In order to continue, it is necessary to return to Christ, that is, the Eucharist.

". . . . Evangelization *through* the Eucharist, *in* the Eucharist and *from* the Eucharist: these are three inseparable aspects of how the Church lives the mystery of Christ and fulfills her mission of communicating it to all people."

The New Testament knows nothing of a system of separated churches professing to be Christian. Everywhere in the New Testament the Church is one - and only one! No one who believes in the New Testament can admit that divisions between Christian Churches are lawful.

The Catholic Church alone has always preserved its unity. We have to face the fact non-Catholic Churches will never secure unity. Of its very nature, Protestantism does not unite, it divides. And on the principle of private judgment and authority, it logically leads to as many variations as there are men.

The division among Christian faiths today is scandalous; and the way the name, "Christian," is taken over by TV evangelists, or mega-churches, can be unsettling because of the tremendous benefits their people are deprived of without the Holy Eucharist. No one knew this more than St. Augustine who wrote that only the Eucharist could solidify differences: "O Sacrament of devotion! O sign of Unity! O bond of charity!"

As "a sign of Unity," and a "bond of charity," the Holy Eucharist calls for Christians to come together again in this great "Sacrament of devotion" to heal all differences and attain complete fulfillment in a world that Satan succeeded to "divide and conquer" as opposed to Christ's "That all may be one."

All Protestants, all Catholics, and all believers of all faiths, whether they realize it- or-not, hunger and thirst for union with God. And it is not possible to become more united with God than in Holy Communion where our love, thirsting for God's living presence, is filled! Christ said "Do not labor for the food that

85

perishes, but for that which endures unto life everlasting which the Son of Man will give" (Jn 6:27).

Every Catholic priest, for 2,000 years, has been giving its members the Bread "which endures unto life everlasting" by changing bread and wine into the Body and Blood of Christ at His command: "Do this in remembrance of Me."

"All things in this world," wrote Francis Conklin, "pale into insignificance when cast in the light of the spiritual, moral, and physical incorporation of the created soul into the very Godhead through the reception of the Blessed Sacrament."

Jesus handed over this great, mysterious Sacrament to the keeping of His Church. He founded this great worldwide organization which would have its ramifications in every country and nation on earth, in order to guard His Eucharistic Presence.

In the early days of the Church, Christians guarded jealously this secret of Christ's mystical Presence as their most precious Treasure. The knowledge of this secret was to them a tower of strength in the midst of a hostile world. It is a secret only to those outside the Church. The world sweeps along, intent on business and pleasure, passes the door of Church or Cathedral, day by day, and knows not that Jesus of Nazareth is there in residence, knows nothing and cares nothing about His actual Living Presence in their midst.

Each day that I attend daily Mass, I am present at the greatest of the miracles that Jesus has ever performed, that of changing the bread and wine into His very Body and Blood – compared to this, the miracle Christ performed at Cana, changing water into wine, is but a pale shadow!

The Eucharist is the Divine gift. Our limited reason cannot comprehend those things which transcend all the bounds of reason. We do not understand the natural order let alone the supernatural. In receiving the Sacrament of Holy Communion we are directly united to Jesus! In his Gospel, the 6th chapter on the Holy Eucharist, St. John reiterates the actual fact that Christ truly gives Himself to us, literally, in the Blessed Sacrament.

St. Ignatius of Antioch was a disciple of St. John and had personal contact with this "Apostle Jesus loved." He is therefore, next to the Gospel writers, in a peerless position to tell us if Jesus spoke literally or figuratively about His actual presence in the Eucharist. In his letter to the Romans, about the year 110, he said, "I have no taste for corruptible food nor for the pleasures of this life. I desire the Bread of God which is the Flesh of Jesus Christ, who was of the seed of David; and for drink I desire His Blood, which is love incorruptible."

Saint Katharine Drexel wrote, "The religious needs strength. Near the tabernacle the soul finds strength, consolation, and resignation. The religious needs virtue. Jesus is the model of virtues in the Blessed Sacrament. The religious needs hope. In the Blessed Sacrament we possess the most precious pledge of our hope. The Host contains the germ of future life."

On October 1, 2000, Pope John Paul II canonized Katharine Drexel who knew that self-fulfillment without God was a delusion. She was born on November 26, 1858, in Philadelphia, Pennsylvania, into great wealth. Frequent trips to Europe for her father's banking interests gave Katharine and her sisters, Elizabeth and Louise, the opportunity to visit the wonders and famous sites of the continent. Always joyful and an eager traveler, Katharine, because of her deeply religious nature, judged all things in their proper value. The galleries, palaces, and works of art she saw in the cities of Europe left her with a feeling of dissatisfaction.

In September 1887, Katharine and her sisters visited the Indian missions in the Dakotas. There she met Red Cloud, the famous Sioux chief, and experienced the Indians pitiful living conditions. When she returned home, she made up her mind to offer unconditional aid to the Indian missions. In four years she personally financed the construction of thirteen schools. This attention given the Indians was coupled with concern for the fate of African-Americans who, despite the official emancipation, were still the subject of unfair treatment. In all the poor Katharine recognized children of God who needed to be led to Him.

For a long time Katharine had been dissuaded from following a religious vocation by her spiritual director, Most Rev. James O'Connor, Bishop of Omaha, Nebraska. He encouraged her to wait and pray. In November 1888, Katharine wrote Bishop O'Connor about the anxiety, sadness, and spiritual hunger she felt in waiting – a gnawing spiritual hunger is a God-given clue to our destiny. In McGrath's words: "The God who longs to fulfill us awaits, inviting us to open the door of our lives so that He may enter in."

Bishop O'Connor changed his mind and suggested three religious congregations to her. Katharine answered that she wanted a missionary order for the Native American and American Blacks – but none existed!

Bishop O'Connor encouraged her to found a new Congregation herself. This prospect did not fill Katharine with enthusiasm: "The responsibility of such a call almost crushes me, because I am so infinitely poor in the virtues necessary." Nevertheless, the bishop did not change his mind and, on the Feast of St. Joseph, March 19, 1889, Katharine surrendered: "The feast of St. Joseph brought me the grace to give the remainder of my life to the Indians and Colored, to enter fully and entirely into your view as to what is best for the salvation of the souls of these people."

On February 12, 1891, Katharine Drexel made her profession as the first "Sister of the Blessed Sacrament for Indians and Colored People." The first boarding school was opened at St. Catherine's Mission in Santa Fe, New Mexico. As foundress, Mother Katharine wrote a rule of life for the Sisters of the Blessed Sacrament. In July 1907, she received a first approval in Rome from Pope Saint Pius X, and, shortly thereafter, was elected Superior General of the Institute of the "Sisters of the Blessed Sacrament for the Indians and Colored."

Why "Sisters of the Blessed Sacrament"? Her insight had grasped that the Eucharist, Jesus' living Presence, is the deepest bond between men, and thus among all the races called to live in the same country and the greatest means to evangelization. "Jesus is the only source of true peace," said John Paul II. "There cannot be hope of real peace in the world apart from Christ . . . How does Christ bring about this peace? He earned it by His Sacrifice. He gave His life to bring reconciliation between God and man . . . This sacrifice which draws the human family to unity is made present in the Eucharist. Thus, each Eucharistic celebration is the source of a new gift of peace . . . The gift that Christ made of Himself is more powerful than all the force of division that oppress the world" (Eucharistic Congress, March 11, 1988).

In 1935, during a visit to the Missions in the West, St. Katharine suffered a major heart attack and had to retire from active life. She lived twenty more years in constant prayer, patiently enduring infirmity. "The patient and humble endurance of the cross – whatever nature it may be – is the highest work we have to do," she wrote.

On March 3, 1955, Mother Katharine Drexel peacefully rendered her soul to God. Today her Congregation numbers 229 Sisters who, in the fields of education, pastoral work, and health, serve the poorest and most neglected among the Indians and Blacks in 14 states plus Haiti, and Guatemala.

CO-PATRONS FOR SPREADING THE CATHOLIC FAITH

A command to go and preach to all nations was given by Christ to His Apostles, and in every age men have been raised up by God and filled with His Holy Spirit for the discharge of this arduous duty, men who, being sent by the authority of Christ have brought nations to the fold of Christ.

Among those who have labored most successfully in this great work is St. Francis Xavier (1506-1552). St. Francis was one of the greatest of all missionaries working for the salvation of souls in India and Japan. He died as he was about to begin his missionary work in China. Sir Walter Scott said of him: "The most rigid Protestant, and the most indifferent philosopher, cannot deny to him the courage and patience of a martyr, with the good sense, resolution, ready wit and address of the best negotiator that ever went upon a temporal embassy."

St. Therese of Lisieux (1873-1897), within a few years after her death became known throughout the world. Excluding Our Blessed Lady, she is considered to be the most popular lady saint in the world today. There are more pictures, statues and holy cards of her than any other female saint; her "little way" of simplicity and perfection appeals to everyone. Great numbers of Protestants have read her life and converted to Catholicism. She was canonized by Pope Pius XI in 1927, who said of her that she was "the greatest saint of modern times."

She accomplished wonders through the power of prayer before Jesus in the Blessed Sacrament where she strived to fulfill her mission – "There is only one thing to do here below, to love Jesus, to win souls for Him that He may be loved."

Always thinking of Jesus in the tabernacle and always thinking of converting souls of all faiths as well as pagans, her advice to postulants were: "By the little acts of charity we perform in secret, we convert souls in distant lands, we help the missionaries and obtain abundant alms for them, thus building both spiritual and material tabernacles for Our Lord in the Blessed Sacrament."

Before she died she made three prophecies that have gone around the world that have made her so popular:

1) "I have never given the good God nothing but love, and it is with love that He will repay. After my death I will let fall a shower of roses."

2) "I will spend my Heaven doing good upon earth."

3) "My 'little way,' is the way of spiritual childhood, the way of trust and absolute self-surrender."

Pope John Paul II said of her: "Therese is a teacher for our time, which thirsts for living and essential words, for heroic and credible acts of witness. For this reason she is also loved and accepted by brothers and sisters of other Christian communities and even by non-Christians."

Both St. Francis Xavier and St. Therese have been named co-patrons of all foreign missions and of all works for the spreading of the Catholic Faith.

Though we can't all be a St. Francis traveling the world to convert countless individuals, or entire nations, we can imitate St. Therese by spending hours before Jesus Christ in the Blessed Sacrament to not only convert the sinners of the world, but to convert non-Catholics to Catholicism thereby heeding Christ's plea: "That all may be One!"

By the power of her prayer before the Blessed Sacrament, St. Therese was able to accomplish great wonders for the Church. She is proof that one soul coming before the Blessed Sacrament is the key that touches the Sacred Heart allowing gifts of His graces and blessings to flow to the whole world!

CHURCH IS BOTH HUMAN AND DIVINE

Mother Teresa of Calcutta knew that the Church is both Divine and human. She was a combination of St. Francis Xavier and St. Therese the Little Flower. Like St. Francis Xavier she toiled in India to spread Christ's kingdom on earth, and like St. Therese she spent hours in prayer before Jesus in the Blessed Sacrament. So convinced was she of prayer before the Blessed Sacrament that she proposed this vital question and gave us the answer: "What will convert America and save the world? My answer is prayer. What we need is for every Parish to come before Jesus in the Blessed Sacrament in Holy Hours of prayer."

St. John Vianney offered Holy Hours daily before Jesus in the Blessed Sacrament, saying, "That is the way to win souls to God." He encouraged visits to the Blessed Sacrament.

No doubt it was prayers before the Blessed Sacrament that obtained the grace for Supreme Court Justice, Clarence Thomas, to return to the faith. He said he regrets having left the Catholic Church, is grateful to be back, and has "found strength by running toward God, not away from Him."

Supreme Court Justice Thomas, who is black, made the comment in a remarkably personal address to judges, attorneys, canon lawyers, law-school students and government officials in Little Rock, Arkansas, at a Mass, May 1, at St. Andrew Cathedral. He also urged public officials to "live up to the tenets of our religious beliefs" and make "patience, forbearance, moderation, thoughtful deliberation, and an appreciation of human frailty" criteria in their work.

"It took me almost three decades to return to the Church, knowing that I should never have left. My mistake was to lose confidence in the institution rather than acknowledging that any inherently good institution can, under man's control, occasionally veer off in the wrong direction."

Senator Sam Brownback (R-Kan.) became a Catholic in a private ceremony on June 27, 2002, in Washington. A former Methodist, Brownback was sponsored by Sen. Rick Santorum (R-Pa.) and was received into the Church by Fr. John McCloskey, who heads the Catholic Information Center in Washington.

Mother Teresa's order of *the Missionaries of Charity* is the fastest growing religious order in the Church and is making more converts than any other. One of their great converts is Malcolm Muggeridge of England who looked into Mother Teresa's eyes and was converted.

Though Jesus gave everything possible for us and to us, He gave us an added comforter and consoler, His own Mother Mary, to be our Mother! While on earth Our Blessed Mother spent most of her days and nights in adoration of her Son in the Eucharist, interceding for the Church. Our heavenly Mother is our advocate, constantly praying for us. When we adore her Son she is there

90

praying with us. "You," said John Gerson, "are the Mother of the Eucharist because you are the mother of grace. You, more than all others after your Son, were aware of this sacrament hidden from the ages."

Our Blessed Mother's first of six apparitions at Fatima was on May 13, the feast of Our Lady of The Most Blessed Sacrament. She asked the three children to fall on their knees and pray: "O Most Holy Trinity, I adore you. My God, my God, I love you in the most Blessed Sacrament!" Her urgent messages underscored the need of conversion, prayer, and penance for our world. She asked for greater devotion to the Eucharist in Mass, Communion, and Adoration. Our Mother Blessed Lady also asked for devotion to Her Immaculate Heart and prayers of reparation, especially the Rosary. She emphasized that if her requests were heeded there would be world peace, if not there would be large scale apostasy from the Church and worldwide disaster! Our Lady requested that a Chapel be built at Fatima for adoration and prayer to her Eucharistic Son.

RE-EVANGELIZE A PAGANIZED WESTERN SOCIETY

"It is not commonly known," said Fr. John Hardon, S.J., "that the early Christians assisted at Mass and received Holy Communion every day. They had to! Otherwise they would not have had the courage they needed to die a martyr's death, or live a martyr's life.

"All the pious exhortations I could make would be wasted if I did not strongly encourage you to attend Mass and receive Holy Communion – if at all possible – every day. I would add an urgent recommendation to spend some time every day praying to Our Lord in the Holy Eucharist.

"Jesus is in the Holy Eucharist with the fullness of His divinity and humanity, and therefore with His Sacred Heart! Except for Mary, He would not have His humanity, nor His Sacred Heart. We may transpose and say, the Heart of Jesus is the Heart that He received from His Mother Mary. She is now with Him, the eternal High Priest ever interceding for us at the throne of His heavenly Father.

"Does the restoration of the Christian family require a miracle? Indeed, a series of miracles. But it is the same radiating Jesus, really present through the Holy Eucharist, who performed the wonders narrated by the Evangelists. Jesus Christ is ready, as He said, to work even greater miracles, like the restoration of family life, if only we believe.

"We have no choice. As the Christian youth goes, so goes the family. All of us bishops, priests, deacons and religious, have the duty to re-evangelize. But the special responsibility for this missionary work lies with the laity – as our modern popes never tire of repeating, it is especially you fathers and mothers, and you children, who will become adults, whose duty it is to proclaim Jesus and Mary to our unbelieving world."

91

HEAVEN HAS NOTHING GREATER THAN THE EUCHARIST

Saint Josephine Bakhita (1869-1947), a native of southern Sudan was freed from slavery at the age of 21 and became a Canossan Sister. What captivated her to the Catholic Faith was the actual presence of Jesus in the Blessed Sacrament, which was her favorite resort, spending hours in adoration.

On one occasion she was left alone in the chapel for several hours. A sister happened to notice it. She approached her and said: "Sister Josephine, how is it? You must have been here for so long. You must be very tired!"

"Not at all!" came the reply. "I have been having a wonderful time with Him. He has waited so long for me."

Fr. Frederick Faber said "One half hour of one tabernacle's Sacramental life is more than the worship of all angels and Saints for ever; for it is Jesus the living God"; and St. Pio, "A thousand years of enjoying human glory is not worth even an hour spent sweetly communing with Jesus in the Blessed Sacrament."

Fr. Frederick Faber again says: "Theologians truly say that the greatest action of worship which a creature on earth can pay to his Creator, is to receive Him as his food . . .   Were we to collect into one all the human actions that have ever been done in the world, with all that was noble, generous, heroic, gentle, affectionate about them, and place them by the side of the act which a man performs in receiving Communion, they would seem less than nothing, a shadow of a shadow. It is brighter than all glories, deeper than all sciences, and more royal than all of the [world's] magnificence. But what are all these ways of measuring the dignity of Communion but like the leaves of the forests and the sands of the sea which we play with when we try to make a little child understand eternity, and which in truth we ourselves understand as little as he."

CHAPTER ELEVEN—HEART OF THE BLESSED SACRAMENT

Nothing delights the heart more than searching for and finding love! To contemplate God's love for me should bring thralls of ecstatic joy to my heart for Eternal love is the greatest adventure of the heart; surrendering to divine love is the greatest of all love stories; fusing one's being with the love of God is the greatest of all achievements of which the physical Heart of the Divine Redeemer is the principal sign and symbol. The heart of the Catholic faith is the Blessed Sacrament; the heart of the Blessed Sacrament is the Sacred Heart of Jesus. In gratitude for the gift of life the Sacred Heart of Jesus should be the heart of my heart and the soul of my soul!

On May 15, 1956, Pope Pius XII wrote an encyclical *Haurietis Aquas* promoting devotion to the Most Sacred Heart of Jesus in which he stated: "This devotion . . . is the highest act of Religion. It demands the full and absolute determination of surrendering and consecrating oneself to the love of the Divine Redeemer. The wounded Heart of the Savior is the living sign and symbol of that love . . . the Devotion to the Most Sacred Heart is so important that it may be considered, as far as practice is concerned, the perfect profession of the Christian Religion."

Devotion to the Heart of Jesus focuses upon his physical heart united to His divinity, as the symbol of a redeeming and forgiving love which knows no limit. Jesus said that living water would flow from His Heart (Jn 7:37-39), and the Fathers of the Church taught that, from his pierced side, the Holy Spirit flowed upon the Church.

The Sacred Heart of Jesus points us to God, as the source of love; a love that is visible in the person of Jesus Christ. It is a love that loves all humanity without any condition. Our assurance of this love was made by Christ's sacrifice upon the cross for the salvation of all people.

The object of devotion to the Sacred Heart is to inflame our hearts with an ardent love for Jesus, and to make reparation, as far as lies in our power, for all the outrages which are committed daily against Jesus Christ in the Most Blessed Sacrament of the Altar – most especially in satisfaction for the many unworthy Communions in the world! Today few go to Confession; almost all go to Holy Communion! To receive Jesus in Holy Communion in the state of Mortal Sin is a sacrilege – a horrible sin!

The human heart is understood as central to a person. It was on every single person's heart that God wrote His covenant! (Jer 31:31-34). This passage from the Old Testament inspired St. John Eudes (1601-1680) to promote devotion to the Sacred Heart of Jesus, and to the Immaculate Heart of Mary, prompting Pope Pius XI to call him the Father of devotion to the Hearts of Jesus and Mary.

93

The Sacred Heart of Jesus is the source of love for men. Because He loves us He sanctifies us through the Sacraments. Of these Sacraments, St. John Eudes said, "so many inexhaustible fountains of grace and holiness which have their source in the boundless ocean of the Sacred Heart of Our Savior; and all the graces that issue from the sacraments are so many flames of that divine furnace."

It is in the Holy Eucharist that the Sacred Heart of Jesus especially gives us the greatest proof of His infinite love. For 20 centuries He has been with us day and night, in the tabernacles of Our Church waiting to give Himself whole and entire to every communicant, to impart to each one His graces, His dispositions and His virtues.

This Divine Heart ardently longs to communicate to us His own charity. "My Divine Heart," He said to St. Margaret Mary, "is possessed of such a passionate love for men and for you in particular, that unable to contain the flames of its burning charity, it must needs extend them through you, that it may be made known to them in order to enrich them with its priceless treasure."

It was then that Our Lord asked the Saint for her heart in order to unite it to His own and place in it a spark of His love. What Christ did in a miraculous manner for St. Margaret Mary, He does in an ordinary way for us in Holy Communion and every time that we unite our hearts to His; for He is come to earth to bring the sacred fire of charity, and His only desire is to enkindle it in our hearts: "I am come to cast fire on the earth. And what will I, but that it be kindled."

St. Margaret Mary, while giving an account to Fr. Croiset about the second apparition of the Sacred Heart, wrote: "He made me see that it was the great desire He had of being loved by men, and of withdrawing them from the road of perdition, that induced Him to conceive this plan of making His Heart known to men, with all the treasure of love, of mercy, of grace, of sanctification and of salvation, in order that those who wish to render and procure Him all the honor, glory, and love of which they are capable, might be abundantly and profusely enriched with the treasure of the Heart of God."

In the last paragraph of a letter to a Sister de la Barge, she wrote: "Let us, then, love this, the only love of our souls, since He has loved us first and loves us still so ardently that He continually burns with love for us in the Blessed Sacrament. To become saints it suffices to love this Holy of Holies. What shall hinder us? We have hearts to love and a body to suffer . . . Only His Holy love can make us do His pleasure; only this perfect love can make us do it in His own way; and only this perfect love can make us do it in His own acceptable time."

For the famed Father Olier, the Interior Life and the Sacred Heart of Jesus were but one and the same thing, that is, the center of all the dispositions of Christ's holy soul and His virtues; the sanctuary of love and worship, where God is glorified and where fervent souls love to withdraw.

Father Olier wrote: "The Sacred Heart of the Son of God is the pearl of great price; it is His most precious gem; God's own treasury wherein He pours all His riches and where He dispenses all His graces . . . It is within that Sacred Heart, within that adorable soul, that first enacted all mysteries . . . See, then, to what Our Lord calls you by opening to you His Heart, and see how much you must profit by this grace, one of the greatest that you have obtained in your life. Let not creatures ever draw you out of that place of delights and may you be plunged therein for time and for eternity with all the holy spouses of Jesus."

In another place he said: "What a Heart is that of Jesus! What an ocean of love is contained therein, flooding the whole earth! O rich and overflowing source of all love! O inexhaustible depths of all religion! O Divine center of all hearts . . . O Jesus! Allow me to worship, to adore the inmost recesses of Thy holy soul, to adore Thy Heart which I have but to-day beheld. I would picture it, but its ravishing beauty will not permit me. I beheld it as a Heaven radiant with light, full of love, of gratitude, and of praise. It breathed forth God; it showed forth His grandeur and magnificence."

PROMOTION OF DEVOTION TO THE SACRED HEART

Through St. Margaret Mary Alacoque's Jesuit spiritual director, St. Claude de la Colombiere, promotion of devotion to the Sacred Heart by the Jesuits became part of their institute, notably through the Apostleship of Prayer (Sacred Heart League), who popularized the Morning Offering and widely distributed the Sacred Heart badge.

It was after Jesus said: "Learn of Me, because I am meek and humble of Heart," that He drew from the treasury of His Heart the greatest of all gifts, the Sacrament of the Holy Eucharist, the night before He died. The following day, Good Friday, after His Sacred Heart was pierced with a lance, He willed that His Heart should continue to remain open as a place of refuge for all. And since humility is the foundation of true sanctity, all our perfection consists in imitating the Sacred Heart of Jesus.

Since in Jesus there are two natures, the divine and the human, and only one person, the Heart of Jesus Christ is the Heart of the divine Person. And "because the divine Person is to be honored with the highest worship; the worship to be paid to the Sacred Heart of Jesus, which can never be separated or taken away from the divine Person, is supreme. This is a Catholic truth, which has prevailed over all contrary errors."

It was in 1675 that Christ promulgated this devotion for all of us, through St. Margaret Mary at Paray-le-Monial, in France.

95

Christ appeared to her in the convent chapel on three separate days. This is how she describes the first Revelation, as she knelt before the Blessed Sacrament: "I felt myself entirely absorbed by this divine presence . . . He made me rest a very long time on His divine breast, where He revealed to me the wonders of His love, and the secrets of His Sacred Heart."

HIS LOVING HEART

In the second Revelation, also before the Blessed Sacrament, "He showed me the Person of Christ in His glory, His five wounds shining like suns. Then He showed me the flames darting especially from His breast. Then He showed me His loving Heart, and to what extremes He had gone in loving mankind, but from whom He received so little gratitude. 'This wounds Me more than all I suffered in My passion,' He exclaimed.

In the third Revelation she saw Our Lord standing on the altar, uncovering His heart. "Behold this heart, which has loved men so much, even to suffering and death, to show them its love. In return I receive for the most part nothing but ingratitude, coldness and contempt, which they show Me in this Sacrament of love."

THE TWELVE PROMISES OF THE SACRED HEART

Here are the twelve promises Christ made to those who love and honor His Sacred Heart, particularly in the Eucharist, the Sacrament of His love:

1) I will give them all the graces necessary in their state of life.
2) I will establish peace in their homes.
3) I will comfort them in all their afflictions.
4) I will be their secure refuge during life and, above all, in death.
5) I will bestow abundant blessings upon all their undertakings.
6) Sinners shall find in My Heart the source and Infinite Ocean of mercy.
7) Through devotion to My Heart, tepid souls shall grow fervent.
8) Fervent souls shall quickly mount to high perfection.
9) I will bless every place where a picture of My Heart is exposed and honored.
10) I will give to priests the gift of touching the most hardened hearts.
11) Those who promote this devotion will have their names written in My Heart, never to be removed.
12) I will grant the grace of final penitence to those who receive Holy Communion on the first Friday of nine consecutive months.

More than three centuries after these revelations, which have been fully approved by the Church, Jesus offers His love to each of us, just as much as He did then. How could we be so blind as not to take Him at His word! After such overwhelming promises, we can only say: "Most Sacred Heart of Jesus, I implore that I may ever love Thee more and more."

The mercy of the Sacred Heart is far greater than any sin humans are capable of committing. The fountain of mercy flows from His Sacred Heart pierced on the cross. "We see that God," said Fr. Benedict Groeschel, CFR, "in His infinite mercy pursues even a 'soul steeped in darkness' that is falling deeper into despair."

In her diary, *Divine Mercy in My Soul,* St. Faustina, speaks of the inexhaustible mercy of the Sacred Heart of Jesus right up to a person's last breath of life: "The grace emerges from the merciful Heart of Jesus and gives the soul a special light by means of which the soul begins to understand God's effort, but conversion depends on its own will. The soul knows that this, for her, is final grace and, should it show ever a flicker of good will, the mercy of God will accomplish the rest" (1486).

It is good to recall how Jesus Himself has recommended the devotion to His most Sacred Heart. To St. Margaret Mary, He said: "Recommend this devotion to ecclesiastics and religious, as an efficacious means of attaining to sanctity, the perfection of their state: recommend it to those that labor for the salvation of souls as a sure help to move even the most obdurate hearts: recommend it, in fine, to all the faithful, as a most solid devotion, one best calculated to overcome their passions, to secure peace, to root out defects, to obtain a fervent love of God, and to reach in a short time high perfection. My heart will abundantly pour out its riches upon all that devote themselves to the same."

THE DEVOTION OF DEVOTIONS

"This devotion," says St. Alphonsus, "consists wholly in the practical love for Jesus. Now, this love is the devotion of devotions. It is truly to be lamented, that many Christians perform various exercises of piety, but neglect this devotion; it is deservedly to be regretted, that there are many preachers and confessors, who inculcate many practices of piety; and never, or almost never, mention this devotion, which yet ought to be the chief one of every Christian. From this neglect it comes that souls make so little progress in virtue, continue to live in the same defects, and relapse even into grievous sins."

Justly, therefore, does that Spouse of the Sacred Heart, St. Margaret Mary, exclaims: "Why cannot I make known to the whole world those treasures of graces, which are stored up in the Heart of Jesus, and which He is willing to pour out so plentifully, upon them that are devoted to Him! By means of this devotion, He intends to preserve souls from destruction, and to establish in them the reign of *His love which will suffer no one of those consecrated to it to perish.*"

"Mankind will not have peace until it turns with trust to My mercy." Jesus told St. Faustina that the Blessed Sacrament is the "throne of mercy on earth," and to daily "Adore, in the Blessed Sacrament, My Heart, which is full of mercy." (*Diary,* 300, 1485, 1572).

One would have to be a hermit not to encounter the evil which is so insidious and pervading in our world today. "Devotion to the Sacred Heart," said Fr. Edward Garesche, S.J., "which is, so to say, a compendium of what is holy and pure, will be an extraordinary aid to parents to safeguard the purity of their homes. The very presence of a picture of the Sacred Heart, set up in a prominent place in the home, is a constant reminder and incentive to special care in regard to purity and edification. Like the picture of the Blessed Mother of God, the image of the Sacred Heart silently rebukes and restrains too great freedom of speech and of action, and where the representation of our Blessed Lord, pointing to His adorable Heart is exposed and venerated, a decent and becoming purity comes to dwell."

CONSECRATION TO THE SACRED HEART OF JESUS

Merciful Jesus, I consecrate myself and my family to your Most Sacred Heart. Through the Immaculate Heart of Mary, I offer you my prayers, works, joys and sufferings of this day. I ask that you accept my offering for the intentions of my family and friends and in reparation for my sins.

Thank you for all your gifts, general as well as special: for creation, redemption, the Sacraments, and for all the graces you have given me. Please join my thanks with the continuous thanksgiving you offer to the Father in the Eucharist.

Grant me the grace to direct my heart and my mind to you throughout this day. Fill me with your love and grant that I may be faithful to your commands, today and always. Amen.

CHAPTER TWELVE—MARY AND THE HOLY EUCHARIST

"There are many ways," said Bishop Fabian Bruskewitz, "in which Mary is linked to the Holy Eucharist. It was, after all, she who gave to God the body and blood that He joined to the soul of Jesus, which He created and then united to His divinity in her womb. This is the Body, Blood, Soul, and Divinity of Christ that we receive in Holy Communion.

"Many commentators see a strong Eucharistic strain in the great prayer of Mary, her Magnificat (Lk 1:46-55). She speaks of the hungry who are 'filled with good things' and the rich and haughty who are sent away empty. She speaks of being called 'blessed' as a result of God's goodness to her. So also in the Holy Eucharist, we, all undeserving, become holy with the holiness of God Himself.

"The wedding feast at Cana (Jn 2:1-11) was undoubtedly a prefiguring of the Eucharistic 'miracle.' Jesus changed water into wine as He would later change wine into Blood. The 'good wine' (the New Covenant) was saved until the last. Of course, at Cana it was at Mary's behest that Jesus worked His first 'sign' even though His 'hour [had] not yet come.'"

Archbishop Fulton J. Sheen once said: "As one searches for the reasons for the universal love of Mary among peoples who do not even know her Son, it is to be found in four instincts deeply embedded in the human heart: affection for the beautiful, admiration for purity, reverence for a queen, and love of a mother. All of these come to focus in Mary."

Pope John Paul II speaks of the powerful bond that exists between the Sacred Heart of Jesus and the Immaculate Heart of Mary, "The piety of the Christian people has always very rightly sensed a profound link between devotion to the Blessed Virgin and worship of the Eucharist. . . Mary guides the faithful to the Eucharist."

Pope Pius XII, who canonized St. Louis De Montfort on July 20, 1947, characterized the new Saint as "the guide who leads you to Mary and from Mary to Jesus." These words aptly describe the God-given mission of this great Marian Saint whose motto was *"to Jesus through Mary."*

Christ lives in all Christians who are in the state of grace. In the great majority the Christian life is only in the earliest stages. Montfort's aim is to develop those earliest stages until Christ has come to the fullness of His age in us – until we have become perfect Christians.

According to St. Louis De Montfort this perfect Christian life is acquired by four means:

(1) An ardent desire
(2) Continual prayer

(3) Universal mortification

(4) Tender and true devotion to the Blessed Virgin Mary

Among these four means Montfort stresses devotion to Mary as the surest, the easiest and the quickest way to the perfect development of the Christ-life in us.

NO ORDINARY WOMAN

St. Basil says that whatever praise we give Our Lady can never equal her greatness because she alone, of the billions of women who have inhabited this earth, received the immense dignity to be the Mother of God! Hence, Our Lady's dignity reaches the threshold of the infinite. "God could make a bigger world or a wider sky," said St. Bonaventure, "but He could not raise a pure creature higher than Mary, for the dignity of Mother of God is the highest dignity that can be conferred on a creature."

Mary was aware of her position as a creature in relation to God the Creator, and although she had been raised to so high a dignity that, "after God's, it is the greatest that can be imagined" (Pope Pius XI), she could find no better way to express her relations with God than to declare herself His "handmaid."

"O Lady," exclaims St. Bernard, "God lives in you and you live in Him. You clothe Him with the substance of your flesh, and He clothes you with the glory of His Majesty." Who, therefore, is more like Jesus than Mary? Of all the creatures God ever created, or will create, Mary is the most perfect image of Christ; and, because Jesus came to us through Mary, it is only appropriate that we go to Jesus through her.

If one wonders why so little is said about Our Lady in Sacred Scripture, St. Thomas of Villanova answers our question: "What more do you want? Is it not enough for you to know that she is the Mother of God? It would have been sufficient to say, Jesus was born of her."

Being the very instrument of the Incarnation of the Eternal Son of God, and, therefore, of our redemption, Mary has been associated with the highest mysteries of the Christian religion. She received graces that no other woman ever received, and in supernatural dignity and power surpasses them all.

ALL LOVE AND MERCY

"The heart of this good Mother is all love and mercy"; said St. John Vianney, "she desires only to see us happy. We have only to turn to her to be heard. The Son has His justice; the Mother has nothing but her love. God has loved us so much as to die for us; but in the heart of Our Lord there is justice, which is an attribute of God; in that of the most Holy Virgin there is nothing but mercy. Her Son being ready to punish a sinner, Mary interposes, checks the sword, implores pardon for the poor criminal. 'Mother,' Our Lord says to her, 'I can refuse you nothing. If Hell could repent, you would obtain its pardon.'

"The most Holy Virgin places herself between her Son and us. The greater sinners we are, the more tenderness and compassion does she feel for us. The child that has cost its mother most tears is the dearest to her heart. Does not a mother always run to the help of the weakest and the most exposed to danger? Is not a physician in the hospital most attentive to those who are most seriously ill? The Heart of Mary is so tender towards us, that those of all the mothers in the world put together are like a piece of ice in comparison to hers."

"The Hail Mary," he continues, "is a prayer that is never wearisome. The devotion to the Holy Virgin is delicious, sweet," nourishing. When we talk on earthly subjects or politics, we grow weary; but when we talk of the Holy Virgin, it is always new. All the saints have a great devotion to Our Lady; no grace comes from Heaven without passing through her hands. We cannot go into a house without speaking to the porter; well, the Holy Virgin is the portress of Heaven.

"When we have to offer anything to a great personage, we get it presented by the person he likes best, in order that the homage may be agreeable to him. So our prayers have quite a different sort of merit when the Blessed Virgin presents them, because she is the only creature who has never offended God. The Blessed Virgin alone has fulfilled the first Commandment – to adore God only, and love Him perfectly. She fulfilled it completely."

"All that the Son asks of the Father," he adds, "is granted Him. All that the Mother asks of the Son is in like manner granted to her. When we have handled something fragrant, our hands perfume whatever they touch: let our prayers pass through the hands of the Holy Virgin; she will perfume them. I think that at the end of the world the Blessed Virgin will be very tranquil; but while the world lasts, we drag her in all directions. . . . The Holy Virgin is like a mother who has a great many children – she is continually occupied in going from one to the other."

DEVOTION TO MARY

Devotion to Mary has always been an integral part of Catholicism. The Church simply follows the example of God Himself who chose her from among all the women of all time to be His Mother – and of Christ, who worked His first miracle at Cana at her request, and who, from the Cross, commended all men into her keeping. "To Jesus through Mary" is a thoroughly Christian sentiment, as well as a most useful criterion for the development of love of God in the soul. The King of Heaven and earth will certainly not close His ears to the requests of His Queen and Mother, and the Mother of all Men will certainly not fail to come to the aid of her children and form them to the perfect image of her Son.

101

By Mary accepting the privilege of being the Mother of God, she gave us Christ. To her absolutely free consent we owe not only the physical Christ, but the mystical Christ also. Indeed, we owe to her all we owe to Christ, because the Incarnation of the Second Person of the Blessed Trinity took place dependent upon her consent . . . ! That consent was ratified as she stood beneath the Cross. For the Sacrifice offered on Calvary, she provided the Priest and the Victim, and with His intentions and desires, she was most perfectly confirmed in agreement. As He offered Himself for the redemption of men, so did she offer Him and herself as well. Consequently, every member of the Church owes the very life of his soul, the Sanctifying Grace won for him by the Sacrifice of Jesus Christ on Calvary, to Mary also. She is the spiritual mother of all men.

Fr. Hugon, O.P., said: "The Blessed Virgin is so associated with Christ in all things relating to salvation, that she is the mother of His Mystical Body by grace, as she was the mother of His natural Body by generation . . . . Hence, it can be safely laid down that she is the secondary cause wherever Christ is the principle cause . . . . Christ in glory is the primary, universal intercessory cause, through whom all the benefits of salvation come to us; Mary is the secondary, universal intercessory cause, so that no grace descends to men except through the hands, that is the intercession of Mary."

Pope Benedict XIV, in *Gloriosae Dominae*, said: "She is like a heavenly river upon whose flood all graces and gifts are borne to us unhappy mortals."

Pope Saint Pius X, in *Ad diem Illum*, said: "By reason of this communion of sorrow and purpose between Mary and Christ, she merited to be called most rightly the Restorer of a lost world and therefore the Almoner of all the gifts which Jesus earned for us by His death and by His Blood . . . She administers the treasures of His merits as by a mother's right."

Pope Leo XIII, in *Jaunda Sempe*, said: "Every grace which is given to this world passes through a threefold process. It is dispensed in most perfect order: from God to Christ, from Christ to the Blessed Virgin, and from the Blessed Virgin to us."

Although veneration to Mary is subordinate to Divine worship, it is not optional. It is a duty for us to pay honor to the eminent dignity of Mary and the unique character of her maternal mission in God's plan; a duty also to have recourse to her intercession and invoke her as the "Woman who in a hidden manner and in a spirit of service watches over the Church and carefully looks after it until the glorious day of the Lord" (Apostolic Exhortation, *Marialis Cultus*, Pope Paul VI, February 2, 1974).

THE ROLE OF MARY THROUGH THE CENTURIES

Before he became a Catholic, G.K. Chesterton once heard an Episcopal priest criticizing devotion to Mary by saying: "It is as though Mary owed everything to God, but that God owed something to her." Chesterton said aloud to himself: "What a splendid thing to say!"

Catholics love Mary because Christ loved her. We love her because we honor Him when we do. We love her because she is so lovable. We can never love her half as much as Jesus did, no matter how hard we try.

Dante wrote of Mary in the *Paradiso*: "with living mortals you are a living spring of hope. Lady, you are so great and have such worth, that if anyone seeks out grace and flies not to thee; his longing is like flight without wings."

Earlier in the *Paradiso*, Dante commented that he invoked the name of Mary in prayer every morning and every evening of his life. In the *Purgatorio*, Dante pictured the penitent souls being cleansed when they meditated on incidents in Mary's life, as they climbed the terraces representing the seven capital sins.

HARD TO EXAGGERATE

The noted English convert, John L. Stoddard, wrote: "The beneficial influence of the Blessed Virgin in the history of Christianity for 1900 years can hardly be exaggerated." It would be easy to document that from Catholic writers. But listen to the words of a complete rationalist, William Lecky, who was also a great historian:

"The world is governed by its ideals, and seldom or never has there been one which has exercised a more salutary influence than the medieval conception of the Virgin. For the first time woman was elevated to her rightful position and the sanctity of weakness was recognized, as well as the sanctity of sorrow.

"No longer the slave or toy of man, no longer associated only with ideas of degradation and of sensuality, woman rose, in the person of the Virgin Mother, into a new sphere, and became the object of a reverential homage, of which antiquity had no conception . . .

"A new type of character was called into being; a new kind of admiration was fostered. Into a harsh, ignorant and benighted age, this ideal type infused a conception of gentleness and purity, unknown to the proudest civilizations of the past.

"In the pages of living tenderness, which many a monkish writer has left in honor of his celestial patron; in the millions who, in many lands and in many ages, have sought to mould their characters into her image; in those holy maidens who, for the love of Mary, have separated themselves from all the glories and pleasures of this world, to seek in fasting and vigils and humble charity to render themselves worthy of her benedictions; in the new sense of honor, in the chivalrous respect, in the softening of manners, in the refinement of tastes displayed in all the walks of society; in these and in many other ways we detect the influence of the Virgin. All that was best in Europe clustered around it, and it is the origin of many of the purest elements of our civilization."

The tradition of devotion to Our Lady is a long and glorious one, dating back to the Apostles.

Protestants and Catholics alike who fail to emphasize the veneration due to Mary are ignoring both Scripture and tradition. As Elizabeth said when Mary visited her: "Of all women you are the most blessed . . . Who am I that the mother of my Lord should come to me?"

Mary replied: "From henceforth, all generations shall call me blessed. For God, who is mighty, has done great things for me. And holy is His name."

LIGHT FROM HEAVEN

Did you ever notice how everything seems to come to life with daylight? It has been that way from the beginning.

The first sentence in the Bible tells us that when God began creation, the earth was a "shapeless, chaotic mass, with the spirit of God brooding over the dark vapors." The second sentence in the Bible tells us how everything changed when God said: "Let there be light!"

Later, when Job complained to God that He was not treating him fairly, God exclaimed: "Where were you when I laid the foundations of the world? Do you know where the source of light comes from?"

In the Book of Revelation, St. John tells us: "A great sign appeared in the heavens; a woman [Our Lady] clothed with the sun."

OUR LADY OF LIGHT

Did you ever notice how light plays such a significant role wherever Our Lady appeared on earth?

FATIMA

When Francisco of Fatima was asked, "Which was brighter, Our Lady or the Sun?" He replied, "The figure of the Virgin was brighter."

Remember how 70,000 people at Fatima were spellbound for twelve minutes when they saw the midday sun whirling and dancing in the sky.

104

LOURDES

From inside the dark grotto at Lourdes, Bernadette saw "a brilliant, golden-colored cloud. Soon after, a lady appeared young and beautiful, exceedingly beautiful, the likes of whom I had never seen."

As Our Lady took the Rosary from her own right arm, Bernadette began to pray on the beads.

GUADALUPE

When Mary appeared to Juan Diego in Mexico, the morning sun had not yet risen. But Juan saw her as though she were silhouetted against the sun because of the golden beams that shone from behind her. Juan described Our Lady as "a young Mexican girl, wonderfully beautiful!" Even the rocks and dry grass were beautiful as they radiated her splendor. Each stone was like a jewel.

KNOCK

On a very rainy night at Knock, on the west coast of Ireland, more than twenty people saw the whole south gable of the parish church flooded with a brilliant light, bright as the sun on a sunny day. Fourteen witnesses testified before the Diocesan Commission that "the figures of Our Lady, St. Joseph, and St. John were clothed in dazzling white."

FRANCE

In Paris, on the Rue du Bac, Our Lady appeared to Sister Catherine Laboure in the convent chapel at midnight.

A little angel came to her room, calling Sister Catherine to chapel: "He was surrounded with rays of light. Wherever we went, the lights came on. In the chapel, all the torches and tapers were burning like at Midnight Mass. Our Lady was very clearly visible. Her face was so beautiful that I could not describe it."

GOODNESS AND LIGHT

Mankind has always associated light with the forces of good. As the moon reflects the sun, so does Mary reflect the infinite goodness of her Son who told us: *"I am the light of the world. He who follows me walks not in darkness."*

THE BRIGHTNESS OF THIS STAR

St. Bernard said, "Oh! You, who find yourself tossed in the tempest of this world, turn not your eyes from the brightness of this star if you would not be overwhelmed by storms. If the winds of temptations rise; if you fall among the rocks of tribulations, look up at the star, call on Mary. If you are tossed by the waves of pride, ambition, detraction, jealousy, or envy, look up at the star, call on Mary. If anger, covetousness, or lust beat on the vessel of your soul, look up to Mary. If you begin to sink in the gulf of melancholy and despair, think of Mary. In dangers, in distresses, in perplexities think of Mary, call on Mary; let her not depart from your lips; let her not depart from your heart; and that you may obtain the suffrage of her prayers, never depart from the example of her conversation. While you follow her, you will never go astray; while you implore her aid, you never sink in despair; when you think on her, you never wander; under her patronage you never fall; under her protection you need not fear; she being your guide, you are not weary."

MARY A BEACON OF LIGHT

"The Eucharist," said Fr. Richard Foley, S.J., "is the great sacrament of hope, and the Mother of the Eucharist is a God-given icon and beacon for us wayfarers and pilgrims heading for home. For Mary is the living link between our sinful selves and the God-Man who has turned all our sunsets into dawns."

PRAYER TO OUR LADY OF LIGHT

"Our Lady of Light, Spouse of the Holy Spirit, enlighten, guide and direct me – into thy Jesus transform me."

INFLUENCE OF MARY

In his outstanding book, *Civilization*, the noted British scholar, Kenneth Clark, commented on the profound influence of Christ's mother throughout the centuries. Though not a Catholic, Clark pointed out how devotion to Mary "taught a race of tough and ruthless barbarians the virtues of tenderness and compassion. She became the mother in whom everyone could recognize the qualities of warmth and love and approachability.

"She was loved and honored as the Madonna and the Queen of Heaven. She was the conduit of divine grace and the mother of us all in a most endearing way. She was the great intercessor who could soften the demands of infinite justice. And she could work spiritual and sometimes material miracles for her devoted clients."

Referring to Islam, and Protestant Northern Europe, Clark noted: "The all-male religions have produced no religious imagery—in most cases they have positively forbidden it. The great religious art of the world is deeply involved with the female role of Mary. The ordinary Catholic who prayed to the Virgin was not conscious of this. He simply knew that the heretics wanted to deprive him of that sweet, compassionate, approachable being who would intercede for him with a hard master. In all these ways, the Church gave imaginative expression to deep-seated human impulses."

106

POPE JOHN PAUL II

The Episcopal motto of Pope John Paul II is *Totus Tuus*: "I am all thine." His mother had a stroke when he was barely six years old, and she died when he was eight.

A neighbor lady in Poland told him that he had a heavenly mother in Mary. He has been very devoted to her ever since, and he attributes his recovery from the very life-threatening assassination attempt on his life to the intercession of Our Lady. The bullet that nearly killed him is now in the crown of a statue of Mary, at Fatima.

He consecrated the whole world, and Communist Russia in particular, to Mary, who had promised at Fatima that if we prayed sufficiently, Russia would be freed from Communist domination and once again be a Christian country.

Vocations to the priesthood are quite numerous, and hopefully, the country will once again be called "Holy Russia," as it was before the Communists took over in 1917.

Mary, the ever-loving mother, never seeks honor for herself, but always wants to lead souls to Jesus, her Divine Son. That is clear as we pray the Rosary, which we should try to do every day.

The Rosary opens up for us many of the greatest passages in Sacred Scripture, from Christ's birth to the descent of the Holy Spirit on the Apostles. The Rosary helps us very much to contemplate the mysteries of Christ's life, and Mary's beautiful life with Him. Scripture also reminds us that "all generations" will call Mary blessed. It is a very helpful way to recall and to better realize her role in the history of our salvation.

The Rosary is not just for Catholics only. It is a very ecumenical devotion, as prayer for all Christians. The two greatest apparitions in the last two hundred years: Lourdes and Fatima, plead for us to pray the Rosary often. Both confirm all the Church has taught about the efficacy of the Rosary.

At Fatima Our Lady told us that peace would come about through the Rosary. She taught us that in 1917, in the midst of the frightful World War I. We can't stress enough that it is a Gospel prayer. It outlines the history of our salvation, and so many of the marvelous lessons Christ taught to us.

Just as Eve was tempted by a bad angel, Mary cooperated with God's Angel Gabriel, when the angel told her: "Hail, full of grace, the Lord is with thee. Blessed art thou among women." Mary was troubled at the message, so Gabriel added: "Do not be afraid, Mary, for you have found grace with God." Mary accepted the message: "Behold the handmaid of the Lord; be it done unto me according to thy word." St. Luke adds: "And the angel departed from her."

Ever the teacher, St. Augustine commented that all have sinned "except the Holy Virgin Mary." Scripture represents the Blessed Virgin as "clothed with the sun, crowned with the stars of heaven, and with the moon as her footstool."

So what height of glory may we not attribute to her! What praise cannot be shown to her, so intimately bound up with God, the Eternal Word, as a mother is with her son! As Augustine put it well, "He is made in thee, who made thee." From the very beginning, Christians were accustomed to call the Blessed Virgin "the Mother of God."

Cardinal Newman commented on the Assumption of Mary into Heaven, body and soul: "Her Son loved her too much to let her body remain in the grave. So there was no long period of her sleeping in the grave, as is the case with others, even great Saints, who wait for the last day for the resurrection of their bodies."

Newman described Mary as "the most beautiful flower that ever was seen in the spiritual world. It is by the power of God's grace that from this barren and desolate earth there has ever sprung up flowers of holiness and glory, and Mary is the Queen of them. She is the Queen of spiritual flowers; and therefore, she is called the Rose, for the rose is fitly called, of all flowers, the most beautiful."

Cardinal Newman explains the great value of the Rosary in these words; "Christ came down from Heaven and dwelt amongst us, and died for us. All these things are in the Creed, which contains the chief things He has revealed to us about Himself. Now, the great power of the Rosary lies in this, that it makes the Creed into a prayer. It gives us the great truths of His life and death to meditate upon, and bring them nearer to our hearts.

"So we contemplate all the great mysteries of His life and His birth in the manger; and so too the mysteries of His suffering and glorified life. But even Christians, with all their knowledge of God, have usually more awe than love of Him, and the special virtue of the Rosary lies in the special way in which it looks at these mysteries.

"For with all our thoughts of Him are mingled thoughts of His Mother. And in the relations between Mother and Son we have set before us the Holy Family, the home in which God lived.

"Now the family is, humanly considered, a sacred thing. How much more the family bound together by supernatural ties and, above all, that in which God dwelt with His Blessed Mother. That is what I should most wish you to remember in future years."

G.K. Chesterton, the prominent English convert to Catholicism, concluded his poem about the Christ-child walking through the fields, with these words: "And all the flowers looked up at Him, and all the stars looked down."

108

The stars don't look down on Him anymore. They look up to Him, just as we do, as He dwells in His kingdom out beyond the farthest star. There we are meant to live with Him forever, in the land that He prepared for those who love Him.

St. John, the beloved disciple, wrote very beautifully: "God so loved the world that He gave us His only Son that everyone who believes in Him may not die, but have eternal life. For God did not send His Son into the world to be its judge, but to be its Savior" (Jn 3:16).

Mary lived a life of Faith. Many times she did not understand, but "pondered all these things in her heart." We too can imitate Mary by accepting and praying about Christ's treatment of us.

When Mary first conceived her Child, she walked many miles to help her older cousin Elizabeth. When Elizabeth heard Mary's greeting, St. Luke tells us: "The baby leapt in her womb, and Elizabeth was filled with the Holy Spirit."

"Why am I so favored, that the mother of my God should come to me?" Elizabeth exclaimed. The name Mary is still the most popular name in the world, and the most popular name for Catholic Churches.

OUR LADY OF GUADALUPE

We are familiar with the appearance of Our Lady to Bernadette at Lourdes in 1858 and her appearance to the three children at Fatima: Jacinta, Francisco and Lucia, in 1917. But as close as we are geographically we may not recall much about her appearance to Saint Juan Diego, a Mexican Indian, in the year 1532 near Mexico City.

As Juan was walking just before daybreak, he heard a heavenly song that he thought was a multitude of birds singing together harmoniously, like one choir responding to another. Lifting his eyes, he saw a shining white cloud, surrounded by a rainbow.

Overwhelmed with joy, he thought: "What can I be hearing and seeing?" Then he heard his name being called, and saw a most beautiful lady, who said to him in his Indian dialect: "My son, Juan, whom I love tenderly, where are you going?" The Indian replied, "I am going, noble lady and My Lady, to hear Mass."

"Know, my son, dearly beloved, that I am the ever-virgin Mary, Mother of the true God, Creator of all, and Lord of heaven and earth, Who is everywhere." She then explained he was to tell the bishop in Mexico City that she wanted a shrine built for her on this spot, explaining: "I will show my loving clemency and the compassion I feel for the natives, and for those who love me and seek me, and for all those who implore my help, and call on me."

After seeing the bishop, Juan returned to the hill, where Our Lady appeared to him again. He explained to her that the bishop treated him kindly, but did not seem to believe that he had seen her.

"As you can see, My Lady, I am a poor peasant, a humble working man, and this mission is not for me. Send a noble and important person on this mission, someone who would be believed."

After listening to what the Indian said to her, she replied: "Listen, my well-loved son: Know that I have no lack of servants to command, who would do what they are told. But it is most fitting that you should carry out this mission, and that you should bring about the fulfillment of my will and my wish.

"So I ask you, my son, and order you to go back to the bishop tomorrow, and tell him to build the shrine I have asked you for. Tell him that she who sends you is the Virgin Mary, Mother of the true God."

She gave him a gorgeous bouquet of roses that were nowhere to be found in the area, at that time of year. When the bishop saw them he also saw the miraculous image of Our Lady on the front of Juan Diego's cloak.

The shrine, of course, was built there, near Mexico City, and is one of the most highly venerated Marian shrines in the world. Our Lady has a special interest in the poor and the sick.

And what of the miraculous image? After 500 years it is still seen above the Altar at the shrine. You have often seen a copy of it. It is known as "Our Lady of Guadalupe."

CHAPTER THIRTEEN—PRAYER TO OUR LADY

Mary is our most powerful intercessor throughout all our lives, and especially, at the time of our death. Saint Francis de Sales said, "Let us run to Mary like little children and cast ourselves into her arms with perfect confidence." Saint Bonaventure wrote, "The gates of heaven will open to all who confide in the protection of Mary," and Saint Thomas Aquinas wrote, "As sailors are guided by a star to their port, so are Christians guided to heaven by Mary."

"The prayer of the Rosary, or five decades of it," said Sister Lucia of Fatima, "after the Sacred Liturgy of the Eucharist, is what most unites us to God by the richness of the prayers that compose it . . . we see that it is indeed a Trinitarian and a Eucharistic prayer, even more than a Marian one. I do not know if we can find prayers more sublime or more appropriate to recite before the Blessed Sacrament.

"Moreover, after the Sacred Liturgy of the Eucharist the prayer of the Rosary is what best fosters within our spirit the growth of the mysteries of Faith, Hope and Charity. It is the spiritual bread of our souls. The one who does not pray weakens and dies. It is in prayer that we meet God, and in this encounter, He imparts to us Faith, Hope, and Charity. Without these virtues we cannot be saved . . . I have great hopes that, in the not too distant future, the prayer of the Holy Rosary will be proclaimed a liturgical prayer, because all its parts share in the Sacred Liturgy of the Eucharist."

Satan understands too well all the blessings which God bestows upon the just as well as upon sinners by the devotion of the Rosary. No wonder that he bears such hatred to the Rosary, and does all in his power to prevent Catholics from saying it. To succeed in his attempt he makes use of his agents – heretics, infidels, and lukewarm Catholics.

Protestantism has always denounced the Rosary. Calvin and Bucer, not satisfied with denouncing it from the pulpit, even caused the Rosary beads to be sought for in the houses of the Catholics, and woe to him who was found with them in his hands. Jansenism, a branch of Protestantism, could never cherish a devotion so dear to the Blessed Virgin Mary. Philosophers who have no faith have always scoffed at it, knowing that the Catholic faith would never perish so long as the devotion of the Rosary would exist. The devil employs both these enemies of our holy faith, and lukewarm Catholics, who call themselves liberal, as his agents, to undermine, and if possible to destroy, this devotion by throwing ridicule and sarcasm on it. They call it *the vain, tedious repetition of the Rosary.*

The reverse of what the devil suggests by his agents is true! The vain, tedious repetition of the Rosary is the most profitable and delightful. Satan

111

always misrepresents the truth; he cannot help telling lies. It requires but little thought to see that the above objection to the Rosary is utterly false, and that the reverse is a great truth.

When there is any question about the repetition of a sinful act, the devil or his agents have no objection to make. They delight in seeing sinful acts repeated because the devil knows that the oftener a man repeats a sinful act, the more he becomes strengthened in the evil, and his conversion is all the more difficult. What is more detestable than to repeat missing Mass on Sundays? Or being disobedient to parents? What about repeating sins of drunkenness, theft, slander, impurity? To the repetition of these sins no objection is made. But to the repetition of prayers, and other good works, the devil has every objection, because he knows that by repeating the prayers of the Rosary, or repeating good works, we become confirmed in good, and more and more like unto our heavenly Father.

The successful man in every calling in life, whether literary, scientific or commercial, is he who can say: "This is one thing I do constantly." When Michelangelo was asked why he did not marry, he replied: "Painting is my wife, and my works are my children." He became a great painter because he was a whole man at one thing. He touched and retouched the canvas hundreds of times to produce some of the greatest paintings in the world.

Thousands of men have failed in life by dabbling in too many things. To do anything perfectly, there should be exclusiveness to that one object, which will make all others, for the time, seem worthless.

This is the first law in worldly pursuits. It is also the first law of success in spiritual pursuits, in the road of perfection. To become virtuous we must constantly repeat acts of virtue; to become patient we must often repeat acts of patience; to become strong in our faith, in obedience, in holy purity, we must constantly practice those virtues. By the same token, to become a man of prayer we must often repeat our prayers – Christ said, "Watch and pray always."

A single prayer of the Rosary, which is recited with devotion, is of more value than all the money, than all the riches, in the universe. What will money, what will all the riches of this world avail us after death? But the prayers of the Rosary will then be of more help to us than all the honors and wealth in the world.

St. Aloysius Gonzaga said, "Diligence in prayer is the perfection of the Gospel." Diligence is being attentive and busy. No prayer keeps one more attentive and busy than the Holy Rosary. Our heart, our thoughts, our lips, and our fingers are all involved.

FROM CHILDREN OF THE DEVIL TO CHILDREN OF GOD

"The Rosary," said Fr. Michael Muller, CSSR, "becomes for the soul a school of perfection, a true and constant nurse of divine charity, the means of her sanctity, and a source of eternal happiness . . . this prayer gives free access to the spiritual treasures of God; it causes them to flow streams upon sinners, and to work wonderful changes in their souls. By this prayer sinners are changed from enemies into friends of God, from reprobates into chosen vessels of election, from children of the devil into children of God, from heirs of hell into heirs of heaven."

It was not in vain that Our Lady of the Holy Rosary has been called the gate of heaven, the glory of the human race, the fountain of graces, the advocate of penitents, the refuge of abandoned sinners, and the consolation of the desolate.

St. Bernard said that Mary throws open the treasury of divine mercy to whom she pleases, when she pleases, and as she pleases, so that a sinner can never be lost if Mary protects him. The repentant sinner is never rejected by Mary however numerous may be his crimes, especially if he perseveres in saying the Rosary.

Queen Blanche, the mother of St. Louis IX, King of France, was asked by a prisoner, filled with sorrow, to obtain his release. "It is not in my power," said the queen, "to release you from your prison, but I will intercede with the king for you that he may grant you this favor." Approaching her son, she said: "My son, pardon this unhappy man for my sake, and release him from his imprisonment." Confronting the prisoner, St. Louis said "I pardon you, but I assure you were it not for my mother you would not have lived to see another day. Be always grateful to her."

By his word God created the heavens and the earth; by his word he changed water into wine; by his word he changed bread and wine into his Body and Blood; and by his word he gave us Mary for our Mother on the last day of his life. He kept this gift of his Mother to us as his last gift. God alone is all powerful by nature but Mary is all powerful by her prayers.

When God created the world, "He spoke and it was done"; when he decided to redeem the world, he left it to the consent of Mary. She said, "Be it done to me according to thy word." And the miracle of miracles, the mystery of mysteries, took place – "God was made flesh and dwelt among us."

THE GREATEST PRAYER BOOK

The Rosary is the greatest prayer book. From the day it was first known, it found its way through millions of homes, even the most distant countries. It has been said in every language throughout the entire world by children, mothers,

113

fathers, scholars, soldiers, Popes, bishops, priests, nuns, scientists, athletes – in what profession is it not prayed?

Over three hundred years ago, the Irish people suffered, struggled, and died for the faith under the persecutions of Cromwell. They suffered poverty with all its bitterness, they endured exile with all its sorrows, and they suffered outrage and even death itself, rather than lose their faith. Priests were hunted down, and the Holy Sacrifice of the Mass outlawed. Under that reign of terror it was the Rosary, the anchor of hope that kept the faith alive in Ireland.

Francisco Suarez said: "You must pray every day for a happy death, and God will grant your prayer every day." In the Rosary we do exactly this when we say: "Holy Mary, Mother of God, pray for us sinners, now and at the hour of our death." And we repeat this fifty-three times every time we pray a five decade Rosary. If we pray the five decades of the Rosary for an entire year, we ask Our Lady 19,800 times to grant us this grace. If we persevere in praying the Rosary of five decades every day of our life, what an immense number of cries for mercy ascend from our lips to heaven in the course of our earthly life, cries for mercy so that in the hour of our death, our souls may obtain admission into the joys of heaven.

In 1972, Msgr. Joseph A. Cirrincione of New York was asked by Sister Lucia and her Prioress if he would translate and distribute in English-speaking countries, a leaflet Sister Lucia had composed entitled *The Message of Fatima – Daily Rosary*. He printed and distributed "about a million copies" to Sister Lucia's delight.

Inspired by the leaflet, he would write a pamphlet entitled *The Rosary and the Crisis of Faith* in expanding on the initial work by incorporating extracts from her memoirs, one of which is from the copy of a letter she wrote to Mother Martin: "Unfortunately, we cannot hopefully expect a great number of souls to assist at daily Mass, but we can hope to bring a greater number of them to recite the daily Rosary. This practice will preserve and increase their faith, due to the prayer life which it fosters and to the mysteries of our Redemption which are remembered in each decade."

THE MOST DIVINE PRAYER

Next to the Holy Sacrifice of the Mass, the essential Catholic devotions that nourish piety are visits to the Blessed Sacrament – a heart-to-heart talk with Jesus – and the recitation of the Rosary, through which we are privileged to hold familiar conversation with Mary and to consider devoutly the mysteries of her life and her virtues.

114

St. Charles Borromeo wrote "The Rosary is the most divine prayer we can pray." "The Rosary," said Bishop Thomas Daily, "especially prayed in the presence of the Blessed Sacrament, is a powerful means of spiritual grace."

Pope John II insists the Rosary is his favorite prayer, and he prays three Rosaries each day, covering the fifteen mysteries. "It is a marvelous prayer," he insists. "Marvelous in its simplicity and in its depth. . . I cordially urge everyone to recite it."

Wrote the late Cardinal Carberry of St. Louis: "Of all exercises of piety, no other has received such praise and encouragement by the Magisterium of the Church."

"The Rosary," said Pope Leo Xlll, "is the most excellent form of prayer and the most efficacious means of attaining eternal life. It is the remedy for all our evils, the root of all our blessings. There is no more excellent way of praying."

POWER OF THE ROSARY

If by prayer, the anchor of hope is cast very deep, it is evident that by the best of prayers – the holy Rosary – the anchor of hope is cast into the very depths of the immense ocean of God's goodness and mercy. The devotion of the Rosary may be called, in truth, the nurse of hope.

When a small Christian fleet defeated the Muslims in the Gulf of Lepanto on October 7, 1571, it was a great victory for the Faith, and for freedom. Credit for the victory goes to countless thousands who prayed the Rosary to protect Christianity when it was threatened. In thanksgiving, Pope Pius V established The Feast of the Holy Rosary.

A century later, in 1683, Christianity was saved from an invasion by the Turks, who were conquering Vienna and threatening to suppress Christianity in Europe. But they were stopped in their tracks, after thousands in Vienna prayed the Rosary for deliverance.

In our own time, in 1955, after Communism had taken over Austria, Father Peter Pavlicek began a Rosary crusade throughout the country. Why Communism disappeared from Austria has always puzzled historians. But we know why: Our Lady and her Rosary drove the Soviets out.

Brazil was saved in a more striking manner in 1964 when its Communist President, Joao Gulart, appeared repeatedly on television, boasting the Rosary could never keep his Communist regime from ruling the people. Nothing could stop him, he thought. But the Rosary did, because it had Our Lord and Our Lady behind it. What happened to the President? He didn't even last thirty days.

Ten years later, in 1974, the Communists took over Portugal. The Allianza de Santa Maria, the Alliance of Our Lady, felt Portugal was threatened because its people had not paid sufficient attention to Our Lady's message at Fatima to "pray the Rosary." So the Alliance started a Rosary crusade in every parish in Portugal.

They passed out Rosary pledge cards for people to sign, promising to pray the Rosary to get rid of atheistic Communism. They collected more than a million pledges. The result? On the Feast of Christ the King in the following year, 1975, the Communist government collapsed. Explained the leaders of the Alliance: "Our Lady saved us!"

Just two years ago, in 1998, Our Lady's Alliance organized another crusade, this time to pray for the defeat of a bill in Lisbon that would have legalized abortion in Portugal. Every statistic indicated the bill would easily pass. Angela Coelha, a leader of the Alliance, said: "We pleaded with people to make an extraordinary effort in saying Rosaries!" What happened? "It was a miracle," she said. "At the last minute the bill was defeated by the slimmest margin."

And what about today? When 1500 bishops gathered in Rome from all over the world last year, they prayed three Rosaries together. The Holy Father led them in all fifteen decades.

You don't have time to pray the Rosary often? The Pope prays the full 15 decades every day. He always makes time for that. "The Rosary is my favorite prayer," he insists. He pleads for a renewal of devotion to the Rosary, especially among families, recalling the saying of our late Father Peyton: "The family that prays together stays together."

OBSESSED WITH MARY, POSSESSED WITH JESUS

Saints are more than just models to be imitated. They are evidence that God is at work in the world – they are eruptions of the supernatural in a world where God sometimes seems to be absent. God raises up saints in each age for His own purposes. This is an age of indulgence, of luxury, comfort, ease – ease of body, ease of morals, ease of principles, ease of almost everything but conscience. This is an age that needs the example of a man as Matt Talbot.

Born in Dublin, Ireland, May 2, 1856, Matt Talbot became an alcoholic at the age of 12. When he was 28, he took the pledge to give up drinking. With the help of God, which he obtained through the Holy Eucharist and the Rosary, he remained sober for 41 years – until the day he died on his way to Church on Trinity Sunday, June 7, 1925, having led a life of heroic sanctity. His mortal remains can be venerated in Our Lady of Lourdes Church, Dublin, Ireland.

116

Matt found in the Tabernacle what he sought in the tavern; in the Monstrance what he sought in the mundane; in the Rosary what he sought in the rowdy. Only in the Eucharist could he exclaim "eureka!" [I have found it!]. He marked off this passage in a book that impressed him immensely: "Jesus Christ is at once the beginning, the way, and the immortal end which we must strive to gain, but above all in Holy Communion He is the Life of our souls." The Eucharist was the means by which he overcame his addiction and ascended from the depths of despair to the heights of holiness; from sinner to saint.

Those who knew Matt best – people who were with him – say he remained kneeling all through Mass except when he went to the communion rail. He remained on his knees even during the Gospel. On Sunday, after the first Mass, he would stay, without moving, for 6 to 7 hours, his eyes shut, and his arms crossed, his elbows not resting on anything, his body from the knees up as straight as the candles burning in adoration on the altar.

Fr. Edmund, C.P., said "Matt Talbot was a contemplative, one whose soul continually turned towards God, one whose mind was absorbed in God . . . ."

He retired in his apartment at 10:30 p.m. with a statue of his two loves, a statue of the Virgin and Child in his right arm. He awoke at 2:00 a.m. allowing him three and a half hours of sleep.

Pat Doyle, who knew Matt Talbot in his youth, said emphatically: "Matt only wanted the one thing – drink." John Monaghan, secretary of St. Francis Xavier's Church, who knew Matt well in his later years, said: "Matt only wanted one thing – God!" In fact, his life was wrapped up in Mary and the Rosary, Jesus and the Blessed Sacrament.

Two of his treasured books were pertaining to the Blessed Sacrament and the Blessed Virgin: *The Blessed Sacrament, Center of Immutable Truth* by Cardinal Manning, and *True Devotion to the Blessed Virgin* by St. Louis de Montfort. Of the Blessed Sacrament he was fond of saying "How can anyone be lonely with Our Lord in the Blessed Sacrament?" And of the Blessed Virgin, "Oh, if I could only tell you of the great joy I had last night (or the other day) talking with the Blessed Mother!" Because he found Jesus in the Blessed Sacrament, and Our Lady in the Rosary, what used to be a dreary day was no longer so – now every day was sacred.

His devotion to the Eucharist and the Blessed Mother would become for him a devotion of Paradise, because it is the devotion which the Angels and Saints of Heaven also have. He used to say, "How could there be fear in any heart that had filled itself with Mary and with God?"

Matt was obsessed with Mary and possessed with Jesus to such an extent that he would bewail to his sister Susan the handful of people there were on earth who really loved God and His Immaculate Mother. Though he loved to speak of his love for Jesus and Mary, only with those who loved God dearly was Matt at all confiding.

Matt reflected frequently on death and the nothingness of all that passes with time. He was convinced that nothing is truly great but only that which is eternal; and, with the statement, "The Kingdom of Heaven was promised not to the sensible and the educated but to such as have the spirit of little children."

His life was centered on the Holy Sacrifice of the Mass. In one of his books he wrote: "Aug. 29, 1909, 19 Masses." One of his prayer books contained a piece of paper on which he wrote: "On the Feast of the 7 Joys of the Blessed Virgin Mary, Aug. 22nd, 1915, I, Matt Talbot, was present at twenty-one Masses." He told friends that he could never get enough of the Mass!

Matt died on June 7, 1925. He was made Venerable by the Church in 1975. Cardinal Desmond Connell in Dublin commented recently that "every time I meet the Pope, John Paul II asks for any news of a miracle that will allow him to beatify Matt."

Unknown, unnoticed, inconspicuous during his lifetime, suddenly important at death, the humble workingman has become increasingly famous today with the cause for declaration of his sanctity moves towards a climax in Rome.

In his book *Matt Talbot*, Eddie Doherty said: "If it hadn't been for the chains he wore as a symbol of his "slavery" to the Virgin Mary, Matt Talbot, the Irish ascetic who may attain the honors of the Church, would have remained as anonymous in death as he had been in life. These chains, found embedded in the flesh of his body when he dropped dead on a Dublin street in 1925, attracted the interest of an astonished twentieth-century world and led to an investigation of his life."

The ex-drunkard, drunk on the love of Jesus and Mary, would become a symbol of all that was opposed to a world drunk on hate, power and pride. It seems as if St. Louis de Montfort was speaking of Matt Talbot when he wrote:

"The power of Mary over all the devils will break out especially in latter times, when Satan will lay his snares against her heel; that is to say, her humble slaves and her poor children, whom she will raise up to make war against him. They shall be little and poor in the world's esteem, and abased before all, like the heel, trodden underfoot and persecuted as the heel is by the other members of the body. But in return for this, they shall be rich in the grace of God, which

118

Mary will distribute to them abundantly. They shall be great and exalted before God in sanctity, superior to all creatures by their animated zeal, and leaning so strongly on the divine succor, that, with the humility of their heel, in union with Mary, they shall crush the head of the devil and cause Jesus Christ to triumph. "

To what did Matt attribute his conversion? No matter how inebriated he was he never failed to pray one devout Hail Mary to Our Lady daily – this one Hail Mary to Our Lady is what he attributed to his conversion. But he said it was reading the book *Hell Open to Christians* that put fright into his life and started him on a life of heroic sanctity.

CHAPTER FOURTEEN—PRAY FOR US SINNERS

We are always shocked by people committing suicide. These unhappy people looked forward to the acquisition of riches, to honor, or to the earthly pleasures or comforts which they hoped to enjoy. Failing to reach the object of their desires, life has nothing more for them, and they terminated life.

The objects for which they had toiled so long and in some instances so heroically, were either unattainable or when attained were found to be miserable illusions. Those who achieve distinctions above their neighbors are necessarily the minority. One man rules, a thousand obey. Riches also are in the hands of the few; the majority will always be poor. No honors or riches ever satisfy those who obtain them. Much less will worldly pleasure produce an abiding peace or joy.

There is but one thing that is wise to strive for; one thing that we may be sure of possessing the means to reach, and which attained will confer a happiness which knows no limit – the possession of God in heaven. Such is the object of Christian hope. There are difficulties in the way; for our own passions, the seductions of the world, and the enmity of Satan intervene between us and our end, but God puts means at our disposal which are more than sufficient to surmount these obstacles. He does more than that, He enables us to convert those obstacles into aids, and by the light He sheds upon our minds He shows us how to transform despondency into confidence even when these difficulties appear numberless and insurmountable. We recognize indeed our own natural helplessness in such a struggle, but by the virtue of hope we are able to do all things in Him who strengthens us.

Hilaire Belloc wrote the following to his close friend John Phillimore, an old Oxford friend, then a professor of Greek at the University of Glasgow, upon his reception into the Catholic Church:

"The Catholic Church is a thing of which a man never despairs or is ashamed. Faith goes and comes, not (as the decayed world about us pretends) with certain waves of intelligence, but as our ardor in the service of God, our chastity, our love of God and His creation, our fighting of our special sins, goes and comes. Faith goes and comes. You think it is gone forever (you go to Mass, but you think it gone forever), then in a miraculous moment it returns. In early manhood one wonders at this, in maturity one laughs at such vicissitude . . . . But the Church is permanent. You know what Our Lord said: He said, 'I have conquered the world' . . . . With every necessity, with every apparition of tangible and positive truth the faith returns triumphant. By that, believe me, the world has been saved. All that great scheme is not a mist or a growth, but a thing outside ourselves and time."

PRAY FOR US SINNERS

In the Hail Mary we ask Our Lady to "pray for us sinners" that we may avoid Hell and gain Heaven. We ask this in every Hail Mary because, in our human frailties, our fallen nature would have us believe that an eternity of suffering in Hell for one mortal sin is impossible, unreasonable; God could not allow it!

But we ignore even a greater mystery. Reports come in almost daily of some one who has sexually abused, tortured, and killed an innocent child. Who can measure the tremendous horror of the child confronted with evil itself? Who can know what went on in the child's mind as it pleaded and cried for help? Who can possibly know the immeasurable suffering of the parents and family members that last a life-time!

To say that Hell is impossible and that it goes far beyond what human reason is conditioned to accept is to completely ignore what we see going on around us daily. Hell is a mystery but it is dwarfed by the perverted abuse, torture and murder of an innocent child.

HELL SPEAKS OF GOD'S JUSTICE

A true follower of Christ has to be a realist; he has to be brutally honest about the consequences of dying unrepentant in mortal sin: Hell – forever and ever – without end! It is an established fact that scholars have often repeated that Christ warned of the possibility of Hell more than He mentioned the promise of Heaven, and that our actions will determine whether we will be "sorted out" with the good or whether we will be "thrown away" with the bad. "So it will be at the close of the age. The angels will come out and separate the evil from the righteous, and throw them into the furnace of fire; there men will weep and gnash their teeth."

The authentic teaching of the Church about the real possibility of Hell is a great help toward getting to Heaven. The Lord's love for us is present in all of His teachings, including His teachings on Hell. But God respects our choices, and at the end of our lives allows us to have what we want: eternal life with Him in Heaven or eternal life without Him in Hell.

"Thus hell," said Fr. Frederick Faber, "considered simply as part of creation, is a very beautiful work. It shadows forth the unutterable purity of the Most High. It speaks most eloquent things of the splendor of His Justice. Nay, silver lines of mercy are thrown across the dark abyss, in that even there sin is not altogether punished as it deserves to be, and also because its vindictive fires are preaching daily to the world and thus defrauding themselves of millions of souls who would otherwise have been their prey. Hell is terribly beautiful. Yet Purgatory is still more beautiful; for it is eloquent of God's justice, His justice

122

even on forgiven sin and on souls whom He dearly loves. It is a more complete revelation of the Divine Purity than hell, in exhibiting to us the Beatific Vision long delayed as the consequence of absolved and venial sin. Then in addition to all this, it is a revelation of love, such as hell cannot be . . . . God's works are so many mirrors in which He allows His creatures to behold the reflection of His invisible perfection and hidden beauty."

DO NOT LOSE JESUS FOR ALL ETERNITY

At the age of 14, Alexandrina da Costa jumped out of the upstairs window of her home in Balasar, Portugal, to preserve her purity and escape from a rapist. She was seriously injured from the fall and became an invalid. She dedicated herself to the Rosary, penance, and the Eucharist in order to ward off Divine Justice for the sins of mankind. On her bed in the solitude of her room she became a victim for sinners. In her agony and isolation, she prayed to the Blessed Sacrament in the nearby Church of St. Eulalia.

She frequently asked the Lord to let her pay for the sins of others so they could escape the fires of hell. As her holiness became known, many people flocked to her bedside. She admonished all: "Do penance, sin no more, pray the Rosary and receive the Eucharist."

During ecstasies Our Lord indicated to Alexandrina the need for Eucharistic reparation. "Keep Me company in the Blessed Sacrament. I remain in the tabernacle day and night waiting to give My love and grace to all who visit Me. But so few come . . . Like Mary Magdalene, you have chosen the better part. You have chosen to love Me in the tabernacle . . . You have chosen that which is most sublime."

Alexandrina's special devotion to the Sacred Heart of Jesus and the Holy Eucharist was rewarded by the Lord allowing her to live on the Eucharist alone for the last 13 years of her life. No food or drink passed her lips, only the little white Host!

The Archbishop of Braga invited her to undergo tests at a hospital in Oporto for 40 days and nights. At the end of this period the doctors were convinced that this was "scientifically inexplicable" as abstinence from all food during such a long period of time is incompatible with life.

Our Lord explained to Alexandrina "You are living only by the Eucharist because I want the world to know the power of the Eucharist and the power of My life in souls."

She died on October 13, 1955, at the age of 51. Her body is buried beside the altar of the parish Church of St. Eulalia in Balasar. Kneeling before her tomb there is a sign that reads: "Do not sin anymore. Never again offend our dear Lord . . . . Convert yourselves. Do not lose Jesus for all eternity. He is so good."

MORTAL SIN

The word "Mortal" is derived from the Latin word *mors* which means "death." It kills the soul by depriving it of Sanctifying Grace, or supernatural life. As the soul is the life of the body, and without the soul, a body is dead in the sight of men, so grace is the life of the soul, and without grace, the soul is dead in the sight of God. The body now becomes a living coffin for a supernaturally dead soul, and dying unrepentant, the soul will be condemned to the living death of Hell for all eternity.

Today we have disguised sin by substituting unpleasant expressions for offensive ones: "an alternate life-style" for homosexuality; "women's rights" for killing innocent babies; "euthanasia" for murdering the sick and the elderly; "sharp business tactics" for cheating; and "living together" for fornication.

Notice that three of the five above mentioned sins are singled out in the Bible as sins crying to Heaven for vengeance: homosexuality, willful murder, defrauding laborers of their just wages, and oppression of the poor.

When St. Louis of France was a young boy, his mother, Blanche of Castile, once said to him: "You are as dear to me as any son could be to a mother, yet I would rather see you lying dead at my feet than that you should ever commit a mortal sin."

When he became Louis IX, King of France, the king remarked to a friend who said he would prefer to commit serious sin if by it he could avoid leprosy: "You are wrong. Nothing is more to be dreaded than to displease God."

In 1954 Pope Pius XII canonized a fifteen year old boy, St. Dominic Savio, who died in 1857. Dominic said of mortal sin: "death rather than mortal sin."

A twelve year old girl who lived those words was St. Maria Goretti. In 1902 she was stabbed to death by an 18 year old neighbor, Alexander Serenelli, because she refused to commit to his immoral wishes. Pope Pius XII canonized her in 1950.

One hundred years later, July 8, 2002, Pope John Paul II, on the centennial of the death of St. Maria Goretti, wrote a message to Bishop Agostino Valline of Albano, Italy, where her remains are preserved in Neptune's Sanctuary which is entrusted to the Passionist Fathers.

After recalling that the saint was "cruelly stabbed" on July 5 and died the next day, he writes: "Because of her spiritual life, the strength of her faith, her capacity to forgive her killer, she is among the most beloved saints of the 20th century."

"In the fact of a culture that overestimates physical relations between men and women," he continues, "the Church continues to defend and promote the value of sexuality as something in which all the aspects of the person are involved and which, therefore, must be lived with an interior attitude of freedom and mutual respect, in the light of the original design of God.

"In the heroic testimony of the saint," he adds, "the forgiveness offered to the killer and the desire to meet him one day in Paradise deserves special attention. It is a spiritual and social message of extraordinary importance for this time."

Mortal sin brings with it both temporal and eternal punishment: "But the fearful, the unbelieving, and the abominable, and murderers, and whoremongers, and sorcerers, and idolaters, and all liars, they shall have their portion in the pool burning with fire and brimstone, which is the second death" (Rev 21:8).

GOD AND SIN INCOMPATIBLE

"God does not scare us away" said St. John Bosco. "You do not have to scourge yourselves or fast or pray long hours. Just do your duty in school, at home, at work; take sufferings as they come – bad weather, disappointments, physical illness, sorrow – they will make you saints."

It is imperative to remember that "Love can forbear," said C.S. Lewis, "and love can forgive . . . but love can never be reconciled to an unlovely object . . . . He can never therefore be reconciled to your sin, because sin itself is incapable of being altered; but He may be reconciled to your person, because that may be restored."

Every second of life is sacred because the stakes are the highest possible – eternity! But God always forgives if we turn to Him and ask for His forgiveness. He is so merciful that He will forgive the greatest sinner, in the last second of his life, if he is repentant. But there is a point of no return! The point of no return is when a soul dies with a mortal sin on its soul – mercy then ceases to exist!

Therefore, God had to create Hell to accommodate those who die unrepentant – God and sin are incompatible! Our words and actions of each day, of every moment, have eternal consequences. "I assert fearlessly," said Fr. Willie Doyle, S.J., "that if only we all prayed enough – and I mean by that a constant, steady, unflagging stream of aspirations, petitions, etc., from the heart – there is not one, no matter how imperfect, careless or even sinful, who would not become a saint and a big one."

ONE VENAL SIN

Even the smallest sin is an incalculable evil! "Mighty oaks are felled by tiny strokes." The tiny strokes are the smallest sins: venial; the falling of the oak tree is mortal sin. The severed oak tree is now only good for fire, or building material. So too the soul that has fallen into mortal sin is now dead because it has been cut off from grace, the life of the soul! It too has two choices: eternal fire, or Confession and building a new life.

One mortal sin can send a soul to Hell forever! The smallest sins are venial sins, and all the venial sins in the history of the world can never equal one mortal sin even though they can lead to possible mortal sin. However, here is what St. Teresa of Avila says about one venial sin: "One venial sin does more harm than all the devils in Hell"; and St. John Vianney: "Oh, Lord, if we only had but some small idea of what we do when we commit sin." How horrible is sin?

Because of one sin Hell was created!

Because of one sin one third of all the angels were cast into the fires of Hell!

Because of one sin the gates of Paradise were closed to Adam and Eve!

Because of one sin our entry into Heaven was forbidden!

Because of one sin we have to "work out our salvation in fear and trembling." (Phil. 2:12)!

Because of one sin a God-man had to die!

Because of one sin we all have to die!

A POWER GREATER THAN SIN

Nevertheless, He loved us enough to redeem us. Why? Because God is love and love seeks to give of itself; seeks union with the object loved, and it longs to be loved in return.

God's mercy is unfathomable and inexhaustible. It is far greater than any sin humans are capable of committing. The fountain of mercy flows from His Sacred Heart pierced on the cross.

Christ said "harden not your hearts." A heart can be a sponge or a rock; it can receive or it can repel. "If the greatest sinner on earth," said St. Therese, "should repent at the moment of death, and draw his last breath in an act of love, neither the many graces he has abused, nor the many sins he had committed would stand in his way. Our Lord would receive him into His mercy."

In the book *The Way of Divine Love,* by Sister Josefa Menendez, the following passage has made the book well known worldwide in religious circles – "it is the cream of the book":

"I am God, but a God of love! I am a Father, but a Father full of compassion and never harsh. My Heart is infinitely holy but also infinitely wise, and knowing human frailty and infirmity stoops to poor sinners with infinite mercy.

"I love those who after a first fall come to Me for pardon . . . . I love them still more when they beg pardon for their second sin, and should this happen

126

again, I do not say a million times but a million, million times, I still love them and pardon them, and I will wash in My blood their last as fully as their first sin.

"Never shall I weary of repentant sinners, nor cease from hoping for their return, and the greater their distress, the greater My welcome. Does not a father love a sick child with special affection? Are not his care and solicitude greater? So is the tenderness and compassion of My Heart more abundant for sinners than for the just.

"This is what I wish all to know. I will teach sinners that the mercy of My Heart is inexhaustible. Let the callous and indifferent know that My Heart is a fire which will enkindle them, because I love them. To devout and saintly souls I would be the Way that making great strides in perfection, they may safely reach the harbor of eternal beatitude. Lastly, of consecrated souls, priests and religious, My elect and chosen ones, I ask, once more, all their love and that they should not doubt Mine, but above all that they should trust Me and never doubt My mercy. It is so easy to trust completely in My Heart!"

Sister Josefa, in the same book, hears Satan say,

"Ah!" he roared, blaspheming, "when I want to keep strong hold of a soul, I have only to incite her to pride . . . and if I want to bring about her ruin, I have only to let her follow the instincts of her pride.

"Pride is the source of my victories and I will not rest till the world is full of it. I myself was lost through pride, and I will not allow souls to save themselves through humility.

"There is no doubt about it," he cried with a yell of rage, "all those who reach highest sanctity have sunk deepest in humility."

St. Peter Damian said, "beware of drowning in the depths of despondency. Your heart should beat with confidence in God's love and not grow hard and impenitent . . . it is not sinners . . . it is not the magnitude of one's crime, but contempt of God that dashes one's hopes."

In the *Diary* of Saint Maria Faustina, Jesus says in His conversations with a sinful soul: "My mercy is greater than your sins and those of the entire world. Who can measure the extent of My goodness? For I descended from heaven to earth; for you I allowed Myself to be nailed to the cross; for you I let My Sacred Heart be pierced with a lance, thus opening wide the source of mercy for you. Come, then, with trust to draw graces from this fountain" (1485).

Even the most unprepared soul of all has reason to hope, for in another passage, Jesus says: "O soul steeped in darkness, do not despair. All is not yet lost. Come and confide in your God who is love and mercy."

In the soul is this reply: "'For me there is no mercy,' and it falls into greater darkness, a despair which is a foretaste of Hell and makes it unable to draw near to God. Jesus calls to the soul a third time, but the soul remains deaf and blind, hardened and despairing.   Then the mercy of God begins to exert itself, and without any cooperation from the soul, God grants it final grace.   If this too is spurned, God will leave the soul in this self-chosen disposition for eternity.   The grace emerges from the merciful Heart of Jesus and gives the soul a special light by means of which the soul begins to understand God's effort, but conversion depends on its own will.   The soul knows that this, for her, is the final grace and, should it show even a flicker of good will, the mercy of God will accomplish the rest" (*Diary,* 1486).

We see that God in His infinite mercy pursues even a "soul steeped in darkness" that is falling deeper and deeper into despair. All that is needed for the soul to receive God's mercy is "a flicker of good will" as "final grace" is given.

ONE SOUL – ONE CHANCE

Christ said: "I am the door. By me, if any man enters in, he shall be saved" (Jn 10:9). He is telling us as plainly as possible salvation is only through Him.

He speaks of the narrow gate that leads to Heaven and the wide gate that leads to Hell: "Enter through the narrow gate; for the gate is wide and the road broad that leads to destruction and those who enter through it are many. How narrow is the gate and constricted the road that leads to life. And those who find it are few" (Mt 7:13-14).

The world of today, as in the time of Christ, tries to pretend that every idea of morality is acceptable to God. In Christ's time, divorce and remarriage was thought to be unfortunate and discouraged. But the pagan Greeks and pagan Romans, and the Jewish religious leaders of the time all told themselves that it was basically permissible. Christ shocked them all by telling them that divorce and remarriage is not merely unfortunate, not merely something to be avoided, but that it is adultery (Mt 5:31-32; 19:9).

On this and other issues, what the world in general proclaimed tolerable before God, Christ said was not. What the world in general was doing was not good enough for salvation. This has also been the message of the Catholic Church ever since.

Christ cautioned all by revealing that a Heaven and a Hell existed, two places that were effectively not mentioned in the Old Testament. He said that Heaven was only for those who repented and believe; Hell was for everyone else.

He spoke of Hell more often than He did of Heaven. When He spoke of both Heaven and Hell, He almost invariably, although the world ignores it, stressed the punishment more than the reward. The classic instance of this is with the Beatitudes and the Woes. If we see a movie about the life of Christ, Christ will almost inevitably be shown delivering the Beatitudes, but never the Woes. Yet, when we read the Gospel, we see that He spent triple the time on the Woes (Mt 13:13-36) as He did on the Beatitudes (Mt 5:3-12). This ratio is even higher in St. Luke's Gospel.

THIRD AND SIXTH COMMANDMENTS

Catholics are hated, basically, because of the evidence they bring against the world that what it does is evil, especially, in not keeping the 3rd and the 6th Commandments: "Remember to keep holy the Sabbath day," and "You shall not commit adultery."

Christ taught a new and strict idea of morality, a strict idea of the Ten Commandments that far surpassed in clarity and force anything in the Old Testament, or for that matter, in any other religion up to that time. He who puts away his wife (and the phrase then implied that she, not he, was guilty of something) and marries another commits adultery (Mt 19:9). The husband may be innocent of wrongdoing in the marriage, but it is still adultery for him if he puts her away and marries another. These teachings are all part of God's eternal law.

Christ's teaching about what morality was and was not, His strict interpretation of the Ten Commandments and His placement of them above everything else, came as thunderbolts to those who heard Him. But those of good will accepted His teaching instantly. His word rang a bell of recognition, of truth, within their hearts.

"LORD, OPEN THE DOOR FOR US"

"Lord, will only a few people be saved?" He answered, "Strive to enter through the narrow gate, for many, I tell you, will attempt to enter but will not be strong enough. After the master of the house has arisen and locked the door, then will you stand outside knocking and saying, 'Lord, open the door for us.' He will say to you in reply, 'I do not know where you are from.' And you will say, 'We ate and drank in your company and you taught in our streets.'

Then he will say to you, 'I do not know where you are from. Depart from me, all you evildoers!' And there will be the wailing and grinding of teeth when you see Abraham, Isaac, and Jacob and all the prophets in the kingdom of God and you yourselves cast out. And people will come from the east and the west and from the north and the south and will recline at table in the kingdom of God. 'For behold, some are last who will be first, and some are first who will be last'" (Lk 13:23-30).

129

"LORD, LORD, OPEN THE DOOR FOR US"

The Parable of the Ten Virgins (Mt 25:1-13) reads: "Then will the kingdom of heaven be like ten virgins who took their lamps and went out to meet the bridegroom. Five of them were foolish and five wise. The foolish ones, when taking their lamps, brought no oil [grace] with them, but the wise brought flasks of oil with their lamps. Since the bridegroom was long delayed, they all became drowsy and fell asleep. At midnight, there was a cry, 'Behold, the Bridegroom! Come out to meet him!'

Then all those virgins got up and trimmed their lamps. The foolish ones said to the wise, 'Give us some of your oil, for our lamps are going out.' But the wise ones replied, 'No, for their may not be enough for us and you. Go instead to the merchants and buy some for yourselves.' While they were off to buy it, the bridegroom came and those who were ready went into the wedding feast with him. Then the door was locked. Afterwards the other virgins came and said, 'Lord, Lord, open the door for us!' But he said in reply, 'Amen, I say to you, I do not know you.' Therefore, stay awake, for you know neither the day nor the hour."

NOT EVERYONE IS GOOD

Christ used strong language. He identified the Pharisees, to their faces, as a "brood of serpents" (Mt 23:33), and "like whitewashed tombs, beautiful to look at on the outside but inside full of filth and dead men's bones" (Mt 23:27).

Even the ordinary words of the Gospels are stronger than anything we find anywhere in the secular media. Even simple declarative sentences, such as: "Those who have done right shall rise to live; the evildoers shall rise to be damned" (Jn 5:29); "Whoever believes in him avoids condemnation, but whoever does not believe is already condemned" (Jn 3:18).

Those who say, "I love God," but hate their brothers and sisters, are liars; for those who do not love a brother or sister whom they have seen, cannot love God whom they have not seen" (1 Jn 4:20).

"Not everyone who says to me, 'Lord, Lord,' will enter into the kingdom of heaven, but only the one who does the will of my Father in heaven. Many [*Webster's Dictionary* defines "many" as "the most, the majority"] will say to me on that day, 'Lord, Lord, did we not prophesy in your name? Did we not drive out demons in your name? Did we not do mighty deeds in your name?" Then I will declare to them solemnly, 'I never knew you. Depart from me, you evildoers'" (Mt 7:21-23).

130

JUDGMENT

Christ Himself declared that at judgment, mankind will be divided into two groups: the worthwhile and the worthless, the good and the evil, the wheat and the weeds: "The Lord called the world a *field,*" said St. Augustine, "and all the faithful who draw near to Him *wheat.* All through the *field,* all about the threshing floor, there is *wheat* and there is straw. But the greater part is straw; the lesser part is *wheat,* for which is prepared a barn, not fire. The chaff shall mingle with the *wheat* upon the threshing floor, but not in the barn."

The only way of being sure of being with the *wheat* and not the straw at the judgment is to serve God now. "He who is right at every moment is right as any moment." No drama ever penned by a playwright has ever had so critical and astonishing an ending as that which we will encounter when our soul leaves the stage of this world.

Conscience warns us now; then it will judge us! No matter how familiar we may be with the idea of death, the realization that eternity is wrapped up in our fifty, sixty, seventy or eighty years in this world is a staggering thought! "It is appointed unto men once to die, and after this the judgment" (Heb 19:27). At that awful moment all thoughts of created things will disappear and we will stand before Almighty God to render an account of our lives! St. Alphonsus Liguori paints a moving picture of the incomprehensible greatness of God Who will judge us:

God is a treasury of all graces, of all good, of all perfection.

God is infinite, God is eternal, God is immense, God is unchangeable.

God is powerful, God is wise, God is provident, God is just.

God is merciful, God is holy, God is beautiful,

God is brightness itself, God is rich, God is all things, and he is therefore worthy of love; and of how much love!

God is infinite; he gives to all, and receives nothing from anyone. All that we have comes to us from God, but God has nothing from us: *Thou art my God, for Thou hast no need of my goods.*

God is eternal; he has ever been eternal, and always shall be. We can count the years and the days of our existence; but God knows no beginning, and will never have an end; *but Thou art always the selfsame, and Thy years shall not fail.*

God is immense, and is essentially present in every place. We, when we are in one place, cannot be in another. But God is in all places, in heaven, on earth, in the sea, in the depths, without us, and within us. *Whither shall I go from Thy spirit? Or whether shall I flee from Thy face? If I ascend into heaven, Thou art there: if I descend into hell, Thou are present.*

131

God is unchangeable; and all that he has ordained by his holy will from eternity, he wills now, and will do so forever. *For I am the Lord and I change not.*

God is powerful; and with respect to God, all the power of creatures is but weakness.

God is wise; and with respect to God, all human wisdom is ignorance.

God is provident; and with respect to God, all human foresight is ridiculous.

God is just; and with respect to God, all human justice is defective: *And in His angels He found wickedness.*

God is merciful; and with respect to God, all human clemency is imperfect.

God is holy; in comparison with God, all human sanctity, though it be heroic, falls short in an infinite degree: *None is good but God alone.*

God is beauty itself; yes, how beautiful is God! And with respect to God, all human beauty is deformity.

God is brightness itself; and with respect to God, all human brightness, even that of the sun, is darkness.

God is rich; and with respect to God, all human riches are poverty.

God is all things; and with respect to God, the highest, the most sublime, the most admirable of created things, and even if they were all united in one, are as nothing: *All men are as nothing before Thee.* He is, therefore, worthy of love; and, oh, of how much! Ah, God is worthy of so much love, that all the angels, and all the saints of Paradise, do nothing but love God, and they will throughout all eternity be occupied only in loving him; and in this love of God, they are and will be always happy.

Ah, God is so worthy of love, that he is obliged to love himself with an infinite love; and in this same love, so necessary, but at the same time so delightful, which God bears to himself, consists his beatitude! And shall we not love him!

CHAPTER FIFTEEN—SOLEMN TEACHING OF THE CHURCH

Hell is the place or state where those who die without the possession of sanctifying grace, God's friendship, are confined for all eternity. Jesus said: "Fear him who . . . has power to cast into hell . . . fear him!" (Lk 12:4-5).

How can eternal torture in hell be compatible with an all-merciful God? God not only does not will us to go to hell, but He also sent His only begotten Son – "Jesus Christ is the very mercy of God made visible" – to die on the Cross that we might be saved from hell (Jn 3:16-21)).

"Every denial of hell," said Fr. Leslie Rumble, M.S.C., "is a denial that God is a loving God at all. God's love is like white light. White light contains all colors. If it falls on an object which absorbs none of the light to itself, but reflects all back to the source whence it came, the object is white, as is a white collar. If the object reflects some of the rays, absorbing others, the object will be colored, red or blue or yellow, as the case may be. If the object reflects none of the rays, but absorbs all to itself, the object is black. The difference is in the object, not in the light which falls upon it. So, too, God's love falls upon a soul. If the soul reflects all back to God, it is white in God's sight, a saint; if it reflects some of God's love, but absorbs part to itself, selfishly, it is not white, but imperfect in God's sight. If it takes all, reflecting nothing back to God, it is black in God's sight. It would not even have existed to be black, had God not loved it. But it has accepted God's gifts only to use those very gifts against God. It is evil and not good. It has rendered itself black in God's sight, opposed to the good God loves, and, therefore, putting itself under the hatred love must have for all that is destructive to good. Good and evil in time have two counterparts in eternity, heaven and hell. And both heaven and hell can be explained only, and precisely, because God is a loving God."

The existence of hell is consistent with divine justice, since God respects human freedom and those who are lost actually condemn themselves by their resistance to the grace of God.

Frank Biegeart wrote: "So long as man is a free agent he must be free to reject the sovereignty of God and God will not compel him to accept it. Man can fight against his own perfection and choose to remain outside of the love of God. The power of choice can be lost forever and this underlies the doctrine of hell. The will can be fixed in antagonism to God."

The *Catechism of the Catholic Church* paints a plain picture between liberty in this life and eternal damnation in the next: "Mortal sin is a radical possibility of human freedom. . . . If it is not redeemed by repentance and God's forgiveness, it causes exclusion from Christ's kingdom and the eternal death of Hell, for our freedom has the power to make choices for ever with no turning back" (1861).

Pope Paul VI, in his *Credo of the People of God*, begins by placing things in the perspective of God's love and mercy, which lead us to eternal life. But he adds that "those who have refused God's love and mercy to the end will go to the fire that is not extinguished."

The Holy Council of Quercy (317) solemnly taught: "God wills all men without exception to be saved, although not all will be."

It is a solemn teaching of the Catholic Church that can never be changed that, indeed there are souls in Hell and they will be there for all eternity. No one, not even the Pope, can teach or suggest that there are no souls in Hell. To believe otherwise is to sin against God and the Holy Catholic Faith.

The Holy Council of the 4th Lateran (1215) solemnly taught: "He [Christ] will come at the end of the world; he will judge the living and the dead; and he will reward all, both the lost and the elect, according to their works. And all these will rise with their own bodies which they now have so that they may receive according to their works, whether good or bad; the wicked, a perpetual punishment with the devil; the good, the eternal glory with Christ."

The Holy Council of Trent (1545-1563) solemnly taught: "But though He (Jesus Christ) died for all (2 Cor 5:15) yet all do not receive the benefit of His death, but those only to whom the merit of His passion is communicated" (Ch. 3, Session 6 on Justification).

Pope Benedict XII solemnly defined: "Moreover we define that according to the common arrangement of God, the souls of those departed in actual mortal sin immediately, after their death, descend to Hell where they are tortured by infernal punishments" (Denzinger, 531).

DOCTORS AND FATHERS OF THE CHURCH

The Doctors of the Church number thirty-three. To be a Doctor you have to have eminent learning, be a saint, and expound upon some truth of Catholicism or defend it. All of the Doctors of the Church are in total agreement that most souls are lost!

The Fathers of the Church number ninety-six from the Western Church and the Eastern Church. To be a Father of the Church you have to have the three requirements of a Doctor plus antiquity. The Fathers too are unanimous in stating most souls are lost.

St. Bernard, the last Father of the Church, died August 20, 1153. The day he died (according to a holy bishop in France, and according to St. Anthony Marie Claret), 30,000 souls stood before the judgment seat of God. Two went straight to Heaven, one being St. Bernard; some to Purgatory – but the greater number were damned.

MORTAL SIN AND ITS CONSEQUENCES

The great John Cardinal Henry Newman of England warned us about sin and its consequences: "So great a thing is it to understand that we have souls, that the knowing it, taken in connection with its results, is all one with being serious, i.e. truly religious. To discern our immortality is necessarily connected with fear and trembling and repentance, in the case of every Christian. Who is there but would be sobered by an actual sight of the flames of Hell fire and the souls therein hopelessly enclosed? Would not all his thoughts be drawn to that awful sight, so that he would stand still gazing fixedly upon it, and forgetting everything else; seeing nothing else, hearing nothing, engrossed with the contemplation of it; and when the sight was withdrawn, still having fixed in his memory, so that he would be henceforth dead to the pleasures and employments of this world, considered in themselves, thinking of them only in their reference to that fearful vision? This would be the overpowering effect of such a disclosure whether it actually led a man to repentance or not."

TORMENTS PREPARED FOR THE DAMNED

St. Vincent Ferrer said that we should all "Call frequently to mind the torments and pains of the damned, and those that are prepared for all sinners. This reflection will enable you to look upon the labors, the penances, the humiliation, the poverty of this life – in a word, all that you can endure for God, as light indeed. The fear and danger of falling into these torments will rouse you to greater efforts to avoid them, and to tend more and more to a more holy and perfect life."

THE GRAVITY OF SIN

If the salvation of one soul is of such importance that, for its sake, the Son of God became man, suffered and died for us, think of the penalty that the loss of one soul will entail that dies with a mortal sin on its soul! St. Robert Bellarmine, a Doctor of the Church, delivered the following talk on this very point to the students at the University of Louvain, Belgium, in 1574:

"Would you like me to say a word about how great is the gravity of sin? My dear people, it is so immense that our minds can in no way grasp it, for it overcomes the faculties of the human mind and conquers all the intelligence of mortal beings. For if it be fitting to measure the magnitude of an offense by the dignity and nobility of him who is offended, then certainly sin, which wounds infinite dignity and nobility, will be an immense and infinite evil.

"What then ought we to think of the disease of sin, which the wisdom, the genius, the power and the faculties, of all men and all angels could never have healed? And clearly that disease would have led the whole human race to destruction had not Wisdom descended from the very bosom of God the Father, and prepared a most exquisite medicine from the very Blood of His own most dignified Body.

"Truly, my dear people, if we had no other argument than this to demonstrate the gravity of sin, this argument is such as plainly to persuade all men that any fault whatsoever committed against God is a crime so gigantic that, regarding the penalty due that fault, we may with utmost justice say: 'Eye hath not seen, nor ear heard, neither hath it entered into the heart of man the tortures and torments which God hath prepared for those who offend Him.'"

THERE IS A HELL

St. Alphonsus di Liguori said: "What is the number of those who love Thee, O God? How few they are! The Elect are much fewer than the damned. Alas, the greater portion of mankind live in sin unto the devil, and not unto Jesus Christ"; and, St. Isidore of Seville: "It is as if Jesus said: "Oh my Father I am going to clothe myself with human flesh, but the greater part of the world will set no value on my blood."

Sister Faustina: "I, Sister Faustina, by God's command, penetrated the abysses of Hell to speak to souls about it and give witness that Hell exists. In the blink of an eye," she noted on February 9, 1937, "the Lord showed me the sins committed in the world today. I fainted from terror! Although I know the depths of fathomless Mercy, I was completely astonished that God permits the world to exist!"

St. Padre Pio (to a man living in mortal sin who did not believe in Hell): "Well, you will when you get there!" At another time, a widow kept asking him if her husband, who died recently, was in Heaven. At first, St. Pio would not answer her. Finally, as she insisted, he told her, "I cannot bear to see your husband in Hell, he is so horrible looking." Although he had made a Confession shortly before he died, he deliberately withheld confessing that he had committed adultery, and so he died unrepentant with grave sin on his soul.

St. Alphonsus Liguori: "The souls in Hell will be tormented in their memory. Never, in the abode of infinite misery will they lose for a moment the remembrance of the time that was allowed them in this life to practice virtue, and to make amends, or the evil which they have done; and never will it be concealed from them that there is no longer the least hope of remedy. They will call to mind the lights which they received from God, His many loving calls,

His offers of pardon, all despised; and they will see that all is now at an end, and that nothing remains for them, but to suffer and to despair for all eternity. The souls in Hell will be tormented in their understanding by thinking continually of Heaven, which they have willfully lost through their own fault. They will be tormented in their will, by being denied everything which they desire, and by having every punishment inflicted upon them which they do not desire."

VISIONS OF HELL

All who know anything about Fatima know of the vision of hell which Our Lady showed to the three children on July 13th, 1917. The horror of what they saw was a powerful motive for the heroic sacrifices they made – they wanted to save sinners from that terrible end. There is no indication in Our Lady's words, as reported by Lucia, that few souls are lost. Rather, the impression is that many souls are lost!

"Our Lady opened her hands, as she had done during the two previous months: The light from them seemed to penetrate the earth, and we saw a sea of fire. Plunged in this fire were demons and souls that looked like transparent embers, some black or bronze, in human form, driven about by the flames that issued from within themselves together with clouds of smoke. They were falling on all sides, just as sparks cascade from great fires, without weight or equilibrium, amid cries of pain and despair which horrified us so that we trembled with fear. The demons could be distinguished by their likeness to terrible, loathsome and unknown animals, transparent as live coals. Terrified and as if to plead for help, we raised our eyes to Our Lady, who said to us kindly but sadly, "You have seen Hell where the souls of poor sinners go. In order to save them [poor sinners], God wishes to establish in the world devotion to my Immaculate Heart. If you do what I tell you, many souls will be saved, there will be peace."

Here is Saint Faustina Kowalska's description: *"I, Sister Faustina Kowalska, by the order of God, have visited the Abysses of Hell so that I might tell souls about it and testify to its existence . . . The devils were full of hatred for me, but they had to obey me at the command of God. What I have written is but a pale shadow of the things I saw. But I noticed one thing: that most of the souls there are those who disbelieved that there is a Hell."* She continues: *"Today, I was led by an angel to the Chasms of Hell. It is a place of great torture; how awesomely large and extensive it is! The kind of tortures I saw:*

The first torture that constitutes hell: The loss of God.
The second: Perpetual remorse of conscience.
The third: That one's condition will never change.

The fourth: The fire that will penetrate the soul without destroying it. A terrible suffering, since it is a purely spiritual fire, lit by God's anger.

The fifth torture: Continual darkness and a terrible suffocating smell, and despite the darkness, the devils and the souls of the damned see each other and all the evil, both of others and of their own.

The sixth torture: The constant company of Satan.

The seventh torture: Horrible despair, hatred of God, vile words, curses and blasphemies. These are the tortures suffered by all the damned together; but that is not the end of the suffering. There are special tortures destined for particular souls. These are the torments of the senses. Each soul undergoes terrible and indescribable sufferings related to the manner in which it has sinned.

There are caverns and pits of torture where one form of agony differs from another. I would have died at the very sight of these tortures if the omnipotence of God had not supported me. Let the sinner know that he will be tortured throughout all eternity, in those senses which he made use of to sin. I am writing this at the command of God, so that no soul may find an excuse by saying there is no Hell, or that nobody has ever been there, and so no one can say what it is like . . . how terribly souls suffer there! Consequently, I pray even more fervently for the conversion of sinners. I incessantly plead God's mercy upon them. O my Jesus, I would rather be in agony until the end of the world, amidst the greatest sufferings, than offend you by the least sin" (*Diary* 741).

In her *Diary*, Sister Josefa Menendez said: "I saw many worldly people fall into Hell, and no words can render their horrible and terrifying cries" (April 6, 1922). "On one occasion I saw a great number of priests, nuns and prelates [bishops] in Hell" (September 28, 1922). "I saw many souls fall into the fiery pit" (October 4, 1922). "I saw souls fall into Hell in dense groups, and at times it was impossible to calculate their number" (November 5, 1922).

In her *Diary,* Blessed Anna Maria Taigi (date not given) said: "Very few, not as many as ten, went straight to Heaven; many remained in Purgatory, and those cast into Hell were as numerous as flakes of snow in mid-winter." On another occasion Our Lord said to her: "Know that at this moment souls are falling into Hell like flakes of snow."

It is good to remember that most souls are in hell because they did not love; they lusted! Love is from God, lust from Satan; love sees the person as a subject, lust as an object; love gives, lust takes; love merits an eternal reward in Heaven, lust an eternal damnation in Hell.

CHAPTER SIXTEEN—THE SURVIVORS

In spite of His admonition, Christ explicitly said that many would take the broad road that leads to destruction; that they are like the weeds that the house-holder permitted to grow in his field until harvest but which he finally ordered gathered up and burned. It is very clear, then, that although Christ died for all men, they are not all saved.

In the first book of the New Testament, St. Matthew tells us that the first word Christ spoke was "Repent" (Mt 4:17). One chapter later He says: "Do not think that I am come to abolish the law, or the prophets. I am not come to abolish, but to fulfill" (Mt 5:17). Throughout the New Testament He speaks of the small number of those who obeyed the law, the Ten Commandments, and were saved, referring to them as "the few," "the elect," "the chosen."

In the last book of the Bible, Revelation, God the Father, through the Holy Spirit, is confirming what Christ said of the small number of the saved in St. John's recorded vision of Heaven after the last Judgment:

"A huge crowd which no one could count, from every nation and race, people and tongue. They stood before the throne and the Lamb, dressed in long white robes and holding palm branches in their hands" (Rev 7:9). One of the elders asked St. John, "Who are these people all dressed in white? And where have they come from?" The elder answered his own question: "These are the ones who have survived the great period of trial; they have washed their robes and made them white in the blood of the Lamb" (Rev 7:13-14).

The word "survived" is surprising. Here are all the saved, the ones who repented and believed who "washed their robes" and arrived at salvation by the grace of God. And St. John spoke of them as survivors. It implies a remnant, a few who made it; and it implies that the rest, the majority, perished. This fits in with what the rest of the New Testament states: that only those who repent of their sins, abandon sin and believe, will be saved. Only a few find the way to eternal life. To quote a few passages:

"Wide is the gate and broad is the way that leads to destruction and many there are who go in thereat. How narrow is the gate and straight is the way that leads to Life; and few there are that find it" (Mt 7:13-14).

"Strive to enter by the narrow gate; for many, I say to you, shall seek to enter, and shall not be able" (Lk 13:24).

"All that are in the grave shall hear the voice of the Son of God. And they that have done good things shall come forth into the resurrection of life; but they that have done evil, unto the resurrection of judgment" (Jn 5:28-29).

It is no wonder that Cardinal Newman would firmly insist that soldiers of Christ should not shirk from "proclaiming the narrowness of the way of life, the difficulty of attaining Heaven, the danger of riches, the necessity of taking up our cross, the excellence and beauty of self-denial and austerity, the hazard of disbelieving the Catholic Faith, and the duty of zealously contending for it."

THE NUMBER OF THE DAMNED

There is a central teaching, which is the heart of the New Testament, that there is a Kingdom of Heaven with moral laws which apply to all men. All must repent and commit themselves to the observance of these good and true laws in order to be saved.

Christ speaking to those who kept these Commandments says: "Come you who are blessed by my Father. Inherit the Kingdom prepared for you from the foundation of the world" (Mt 25:34). But to those who do not keep these Commandments: "Depart from me you accursed, into the everlasting fire prepared for the Devil and his angels" (Mt 25:41).

The April, 1995, issue of *Homiletic and Pastoral Review* carried an article titled: "Do Many People go to Hell?" The captivating article concluded by saying that "with all of the serious sins in the world today it is likely that many go to Hell!"

Our Lord, Our Lady, and all the saints and blessed, from time immemorial, who are recorded as having spoken about the relative numbers of the elect and the damned have unanimously agreed that few are saved. Here is a sampling of the more famous:

Our Lord: the saved are the "few," the "chosen," the "elect."

Our Lady of Fatima: "Many souls go to Hell."

St. Peter: "If the just man shall scarcely be saved, where shall the ungodly and the sinner appear?" (1 Pt 4:18).

St. Thomas Aquinas: "There are a few who are saved."

St. Augustine: "Beyond a doubt the elect are few."

St. John Vianney: "The number of the saved is as few as the number of grapes left after the vineyard pickers have passed."

St. Louis de Montfort: "The number of the elect is so small – so small – that were we to know how small it is, we should faint away with grief."

St. Philip Neri: "So vast a number of miserable souls perish, and so comparatively few are saved."

St. Teresa of Avilla: "Souls are falling into Hell like leaves from the trees."

St. Joseph Benedict Labre: "Many will be damned; few will be saved."

St. John of the Cross: "Behold how many that are called, and how few that are chosen. And see that if you have no care for yourself, your perdition is

140

more certain than your amendment, especially since the way that leads to eternal life is so narrow."

St. John Chrysostom: "In our city [Antioch; population, 100,000], among so many thousands, scarcely can one hundred be found who will be saved, for in the youngsters is great wickedness, and in the elders deadness."

Pope St. Gregory the Great: "There are many who arrive at the faith, but few that are led into the heavenly kingdom."

Origen: "They are few, not many, who enter in at the narrow gate and find the strait way that leads to life eternal."

St. Justin Martyr: "The majority of men shall not see God, excepting those who live justly, purified by righteousness and by every other virtue."

St. Anselm: "If you would be certain of being in the number of the Elect, strive to be one of the few, not one of the many. And if you would be quite sure of your salvation, strive to be among the fewest of the few; that is to say: do not follow the great majority of mankind, but follow those who enter upon the narrow way, who renounce the world, who give themselves to prayer, and who never relax their efforts by day or by night, so that they may attain everlasting blessedness."

St. John Climacus: "Live with the few if you would reign with the few."

St. Robert Bellarmine: "For the good Christians there is eternal life full of every happiness and free from every sort of evil; as, on the contrary, for the infidels and for the bad Christians there is eternal death full of every misery and deprived of every good."

St. Jerome: "Many begin well, but few there are who persevere. In order that you may better appreciate the meaning of Our Lord's words, and perceive more clearly how few are the Elect, observe that Christ did not say that those were few in number who walked the path to Heaven, but that there were but few who found the narrow way, so overgrown, so dark and difficult to discern, that there are many who never find it their whole life long. And those who do find it are constantly exposed to the danger of deviating from it, of mistaking their way and unwittingly wandering away from it."

St. Bede: "Nor should we think that it is enough for salvation that we are no worse off than the mass of careless and indifferent or that in our faith we are, like so many others, uninstructed."

St. Robert Southwell: "The worldlings are deceived who think to go to Heaven by the wide way that only leads to perdition! The path to heaven is narrow; therefore assured is their ruin who, after the testimony of so many thousands of saints, will not learn."

Blessed Angela de Foligno: "There are many who before men seem to be saved, who before God are already reprobate."

141

St. Anthony Mary Claret: "You may say that the sinner does not think of Hell, nor even believes in it. So much the worse for him. Do you by any chance think that he will not be condemned because of his unbelief? Certainly not, for it is a most manifest sign of his fatal condemnation as the Gospel says: (Mk 16:16). Although the sinner does not believe in Hell, he shall nevertheless go there if he has the misfortune to die in mortal sin, even though he neither believes in Hell nor even thinks about it."

St. Francis Xavier: "Behold, Lord, how to the dishonor of Thy name, Hell is peopled with them [infidels]!"

St. Alphonsus de Liguori: "Everyone desires to be saved but the greater part is lost." And, "The saved are few, but we must live with the few if we would be saved with the few. O God, too few indeed they are: yet amongst those few I wish to be."

St. Vincent de Paul: "A great number of persons live in the state of damnation!"

St. Remigius: "Few Christian adults are saved, and the rest are damned for sins of impurity."

St. Leonard of Port Maurice: "A great number of Christians are lost."

St. Veronica Giuliani: "The number of the damned is incalculable."

Blessed Anna Maria Taigi: "The greater number of Christians today are damned."

St. Anthony: "Their strongest desire [in Hell] will be to die." "Men shall seek death and shall not find it. And they shall desire to die, and death shall fly from them" (Apoc. 9:6).

Fr. Segneri: "Three-fourths of the reprobate are damned for sins of impurity."

Salivan: "How is it that men believe in death, judgment, hell, and eternity, and yet live without fearing them? Hell is believed, and yet how many go down there!"

Sister Lucy of Fatima: "Only a small part of the human race will be saved."

Jacinta of Fatima: "Oh, so many souls go to Hell, so many souls go to Hell!"

St. Peter Damian: "Go on sinner, go on, unchaste one; give thy flesh its desires: a day will come when thy impurities will be to thee as pitch within thy bowels, to nourish the fire which consumes."

THE MOST TERRIFYING WORDS EVER SPOKEN
We are preparing ourselves for the ultimate mystery, the ultimate wonder, and the ultimate discovery, that "No eye has seen, no ear heard, nor has it entered

142

into the heart of man what God has prepared for those who love Him" (1 Cor 2:9). Words pale into insignificance when contemplating the all loving, all knowing, all powerful God. Our Lord's words speak volumes: "No one can see me and live!"

Only in the resurrected body can this come to fruition. St. Paul tells us that the risen body will be imperishable, glorious, powerful and spiritual (1 Cor 15:42-44). The risen body, now glorified, will have four gifts: impassibility, splendor, agility, and subtlety.

Impassibility means our risen bodies will never know physical pain or corruption; splendor is the ability to shine with a glory like that of Jesus at the Transfiguration; agility is the capacity to pass from place to place with the speed of thought, and subtlety enables these bodies to interpenetrate other material things and pass through them as Christ passed through the barred door in the Upper Room of Jerusalem (Jn 20:19).

Throughout all eternity the damned souls can never be with their Creator or know these gifts! In place of impassibility their risen bodies will know pain; in place of splendor their bodies will be bronze and black with fire; in place of agility, they will be restricted to the confines of Hell; and in place of subtlety, they can not even break the bonds that lock them in Hell!

Hell is where the damned souls will realize, too late, what their sin cost them! Therefore, "It is the greatest of errors," said St. Eucherius, "to neglect the business of eternal salvation."

"We will all be changed, in a moment, in the twinkling of an eye, at the last trumpet. For the trumpet will sound, and the dead will be raised imperishable, and we will be changed" (1 Cor 15:51-52).

Then Jesus Christ will be our judge! And He said that Judgment Day is not going to be a day of rejoicing but a day of general mourning. On Judgment Day Our Lord will say to those about to be damned the most terrifying words imaginable: "Depart from me you cursed into everlasting fire which was prepared for the devil and his angels" (Mt 25:41).

CHAPTER SEVENTEEN—THERE IS A MORAL LAW

In every person there is a sense of right and wrong. Every person knows when he is going against an inward voice. It is the voice of conscience dictating to us a law we did not make, and which no man could have made, for this voice protests whether other men know our conduct or not. This voice warns us beforehand and condemns us after we violate it. The law dictated by this voice of conscience is from God who has written his law in our hearts.

The great minds of Paganism were believers in the existence of Conscience and the Moral Law.

Cicero (106 – 43 B.C.), a Roman statesman and philosopher speaks of that Moral Law which "no nation can overthrow or annul. Neither a senate nor a whole people can relieve us from its injunctions. It is the same in Athens and in Rome; the same yesterday, to-day and for ever."

Seneca (4 B.C. – 65 A.D.), a Roman philosopher and statesman, wrote: "Every man has a judge and witness within himself of all the good and evil that he does . . . . The foundation of true joy is in the conscience . . . . God is nigh to thee, he is with thee, he is within thee. . . . A sacred spirit is resident in us, an observer and guardian both of what is good and what is evil in us."

Epictetus (60 A.D. – 120 A.D.), a Greek philosopher, declared: "When we are children, our parents deliver us to the care of a tutor . . . . When we are become men, God delivers us to the guardianship of an implanted conscience. If you always remember that God stands by, as a witness of whatever you do, either in soul or body, you will never err, either in your prayers or actions, and you will have God abiding with you. Never say, when you have shut your door and darkened your room, you are alone; for you are not alone, but God is within, and your genius is within; and what need have they of a light to see what you are doing?"

Aristotle (384 – 322 B.C.), a Greek Philosopher, said that man is a moral being, able to distinguish between good and evil, justice and injustice; in other words, that the final bases of right and duty are to be found in a perception of the eternal distinctions between right and wrong; and if so, then the Moral Law is something independent of the amount of time a person lives on this earth.

Juvenal (60 - 140 A.D.), a Roman satirical poet, wrote: "By the verdict of his own breast no guilty man is ever acquitted."

Christ gave us the test of our love for Him when He said: "If you love me, keep my Commandments" (Jn 14:15). Just as the Apostles Creed is a concise summary of the faith, so the Ten Commandments of God are a concise summary of morals. They are an explicit statement of the natural laws of truth, order and justice.

Because God made them for all men and for all time, they are holy, just, true and unchangeable. They are a light on the pilgrimage of men through the dark valley of this life of trial, and if they are observed, they will bring happiness, even on this side of the grave. It is not sufficient to believe God's revelation; we must also do what He tells us.

1. I am the Lord thy God. Thou shall not have strange gods before Me.
2. Thou shall not take the name of the Lord thy God in vain.
3. Remember to keep holy the Sabbath day.
4. Honor thy father and thy mother.
5. Thou shall not kill.
6. Thou shall not commit adultery.
7. Thou shall not steal.
8. Thou shall not bear false witness against thy neighbor.
9. Thou shall not covet thy neighbor's wife.
10. Thou shall not covet thy neighbor's goods.

What plainer words could Jesus have spoken when he said it was not enough to have faith in him; we also must obey his commandments! "Why do you call me 'Lord, Lord,' but do not do the things I command?" (Lk 6:46, Mt 7:21-23, 19:16-21); and, "The way we may be sure that we know him is to keep his commandments. Whoever says, 'I know him,' but does not keep his commandments is a liar, and the truth is not in him" (1 Jn 2:3-4, 3:19-24, 5:3-4).

Luther promised salvation to "all who accept Christ as their Savior." If one is saved by accepting Christ as one's Savior, then there is no real need to repent! Yet, the essence of Christ's message can be expressed briefly, "Repent for the Kingdom of Heaven is at hand" (Mt 4:17). The Ten Commandments must be obeyed!

Cardinal John Henry Newman said: "Let us not deceive ourselves. There are not two ways of salvation, a broad and narrow way. The world chooses the broad way and, in consequence, hates and spurns the narrow way. Our blessed Lord has chosen for us the narrow way and teaches us to denounce and scorn the broad way."

Fr. Robert D. Smith mentions ten common excuses people will offer today and refutes each one:

First: In his own time, many of His opponents thought that they were free of the call to repentance if they were descendants of Abraham. Jesus said to them, "If you were children of Abraham, you would be doing the works of Abraham" (Jn 8:39).

146

Second: Today, many say, "I am a friend of Christ, and therefore I am excused from obedience to the laws of the Kingdom of Heaven, obedience to the Ten Commandments." Christ says, "Not everyone who says to me, 'Lord, Lord,' will enter the Kingdom of Heaven, but only the one who does the will of my Father in Heaven" (Mt 7:21).

Third: Many say, "I may be an adulterer, or I may be a thief, but I mean well, I have a good heart." Christ says, "A good tree does not bear rotten fruit" (Lk 6:43).

Fourth: Many say, "I intend to repent later on." Christ says, "If that wicked servant says to himself, 'My master is long delayed, and begins to beat his fellow servants . . . that servant's master will come on an unexpected day ... and will punish him severely" (Mt 24: 48-51).

Fifth: Many say, "I have many good points to compensate for sin." Christ said, as above, "A good tree does not bear rotten fruit" (Lk 6:43). In such a case, even what seem to be good works become only a façade to win social acceptance.

Sixth: Many say, "I was born this way." Christ says, "Whoever denies me before men, I will deny before my heavenly Father" (Mt 10:33).

Seventh: Many say, "Christianity is all about love, therefore, God cannot possibly punish anyone." Christ says, as above, "Whoever denies me before men, I will deny before my heavenly Father" (Mt 10:23).

Eighth: Many say, "The fact that I do not believe in Hell guarantees me that I cannot possibly go there." Christ says, "Whoever believes and is baptized will be saved; whoever does not believe will be condemned" (Mk 16:16).

Ninth: Many say, "I have a good reason, a good excuse, for rejecting the call to repentance." Christ says, "One by one they all began to excuse themselves . . . I tell you none of those men who were invited will taste my dinner" (Lk 14:18,24).

Tenth: Many say, "I am waiting to hear a preacher or an apostle who can overwhelm me with a totally charming manner and presentation." Christ said to the 72 disciples, "Whoever listens to you listens to me. Whoever rejects you rejects me. And whoever rejects me rejects the one who sent me" (Lk 10:16).

The purpose then of all Christian preaching, in other words, is not to explain why certain thing are evil, but to explain why all excuses and reasons for doing them, so seemingly plausible because of the vast numbers of people who straight-facedly present them as valid, are totally worthless.

Pope Pius IX, who issued his famous *Syllabus* condemning the errors and heresies of the modern world, used to ask preachers to preach more often on the four last things, especially on Hell, as he himself did preach. He asked this because the thought of Hell makes saints.

Christ and His Church, the New Testament and Tradition, have always taught that the saved are "the elect," "the chosen," "the few"; that Judgment Day is not at all a day of general rejoicing but a day of wrath, of general "mourning."

AMCHURCH COMES OUT

In his book *Amchurch Comes Out,* Paul Likoudis quotes Sylvia MacEachern, editor of *The Orator*, an independent Catholic newsletter (pages 119-120): "At precisely the same time that the Canadian bishops, at the prompting of the Canadian Conference of Catholic Bishops' English Office of Liturgy – headed by bishop, later cardinal, G. Emmett Carter – decreed the vernacular, turned the altars around, instructed their people to receive Communion standing, in the hand – all of this years before Pope Paul VI decreed the Novus Ordo – the bishops sent a letter to Canadian Justice Minister and future Prime Minister Pierre Elliott Trudeau supporting his proposals for the decriminalization of abortion, divorce, contraception, and homosexuality.

"That same year appeared the Canadian Catechism, which said nothing about the Ten Commandments, the precepts of the Church, original sin, the divinity of Christ, the Real Presence, the Sacrifice of the Mass, the Immaculate Conception, the Virgin Birth, the sacraments, the infallibility of the Pope; but it did say a lot about the 'spirit of Vatican II.'

"Not coincidentally, 1966, is also the year the Canadian bishops made the sex education of children a priority in their Catholic schools.

"Sylvia MacEachern's research into Canada's liturgical establishment began in early 1999 when a lawsuit alleging sexual abuse was filed against prominent Canadian liturgist Fr. Barry Glendinning, a priest of the Diocese of London, Ontario.

"'I started interviewing Glendinning's victims and their families,'" she told *The Wanderer,* "'and others who knew him, and when I saw these allegations go back decades, I started reading his material. What struck me was his great aversion to the Real Presence, and I was reminded of an old article from the *Dublin Review* which observed that Queen Elizabeth refused to stay at Mass if the Host were elevated.'"

AN IMAGE OF SPIRITUAL DEATH

Pope John Paul II walked into a meeting of American bishops this spring and without any of the formalities of introduction stared at the bishops asking, "What is going on in the U.S.?" as reported in *The National Catholic Register* April 21-27, 2002. Wade A. Chio, in his article *Time For All Catholics To Get*

On Their Knees, (*The Wanderer,* July 18, 2002) said: "From all evidence, the majority of Catholics practice contraception by one method or another. Our divorce rate was once an enviable 15%; now it is 50%. A substantial portion of the Church supports a so-called pro-choice position, including some highly public Catholic figures. As a result our abortion rate parallels that of society taken as a whole. Seventy percent of Catholics do not believe in the real presence of Our Lord's Body and Blood in the Eucharist. The percentage of Catholics receiving Holy Communion unworthily, that is, in a state of mortal sin, is staggering. In some dioceses 70% of Catholics fail to attend Sunday Mass. Even in the best diocese, only 65% attend Sunday Mass. We come to Christ's banquet late, in garments unfit for the occasion, and leave before praying and singing in thanksgiving to God in our rush to get out the door. Many who miss Mass wouldn't think twice about going to Communion without going to Confession. A priest conducting a premarital class was shocked to discover that all but one of the couples was living together.

"These statistics paint an image of spiritual death; certainly not the narrow road which Christ calls His Church to walk . . . .

"God warned His people Israel not to take on the practices of the people around them. They did anyway. The result was destruction and exile. In one generation we have managed to take on all of the characteristics of the people around us, just like the Jews of old. Normal in America has become the center-line stripe on the road to Hell.

"The Church in America, from cardinals to laity, needs to get on our collective knees, examine our lives and confess our sins, participating in prayer before our Lord in perpetual adoration."

EVERYTHING PASSES HERE ON EARTH

Born on January 5, 1846, and beatified by Pope John Paul II on November 13, 1983, Mariam Baouardy, a Carmelite cloistered nun was called "The Little Arab." Her family was Lebanese, originally from Damascus, of the Greek-Melkite Catholic rite. When both of her parents died, while she was barely three years of age, her paternal uncle Ibillin adopted her. Later Mariam was welcomed by a Moslem family who gradually tried to convert her to Islam. Loudly she proclaimed her faith in Jesus: "Moslem, no, never! I am a daughter of the Catholic, Apostolic, Roman Church, and I hope by the grace of God to persevere until my death in my religion, which is the only true one."

She became a Carmelite known as Sister Mary of Jesus Crucified and was professed on November 21, 1871. She had the stigmata of her crucified

Savior, experienced levitation, the knowledge of hearts, prophecies, and facial radiance. Frequently she would repeat, "Everything passes here on earth. What are we? Nothing but dust, nothingness, and God is so great, so beautiful, so lovable and He is not loved."

She had an intense devotion to the Holy Spirit. She sent a message to Pope Pius IX that the Church, even in seminaries, is neglecting true devotion to the Holy Spirit. Her prayer to the Holy Spirit was: "Holy Spirit, inspire me. Love of God consume me. Along the true road, lead me. Mary, my mother, look down upon me. With Jesus, bless me. From all evil, from all illusion, from all danger, preserve me." This simple prayer has gone around the world.

Rene Schwob, a Jewish Catholic, wrote of her: "Shortly before the time in which blossomed – we might add miraculously sheltered – the pure sanctity of Therese of the Child Jesus at Lisieux and of Elizabeth of the Trinity at Dijon, there unfolded at Pau, Mangalore and then at Bethlehem, one of the most wonderful lives in the history of Catholicism, that of a little Arab, Mariam Baourdy, in religion Sister Mary of Jesus Crucified."

Reverend Amedee Brunot, S.C.J., the author of the book *Mariam – The Little Arab* answers very clearly the relevance of Blessed Mary of Jesus Crucified to the whole world at the start of the third millennium in these words: "While we follow the mystical crescendo of her life, we shall see three major themes emerge: she affirms and reveals the reality of the supernatural world, the transcendence of the love of God, and the activity of the Holy Spirit in the Church" . . . "What is more astonishing than the trajectory of a saint? What greater message of hope could there be today in the troubled Near East and to tell the Palestinians: here is a young girl of your race, your language and one of your most honored rites?"

Sister Mary of Jesus Crucified was instrumental in the founding of a Carmel in Mangalore, India, in 1871, and in 1875, in Bethlehem of Palestine. She died at the age of 33 on August 26, 1878, in Bethlehem.

THE POWER OF PRAYER FOR SOULS

Dina Belanger, beatified by Pope John Paul II, was a Canadian woman devoted to prayer before the Blessed Sacrament. Before her holy hour Jesus would show her multitudes of souls on the precipice of Hell. She would see these same souls in the hands of God after her holy hour. Jesus gave blessed Dina a message to give to the Church. The value of a holy hour is so great that it brings multitudes of souls from the edge and brink of Hell to the very gates of Heaven.

"This is truly a tremendous mystery," said Pope Pius XII, "upon which we can never meditate enough – that the salvation of many souls depends on the prayers and voluntary mortifications offered for that intention by the members of the mystical body of Jesus Christ."

Quoting Our Lord, Rev. Peter J. Arnoudt, S.J., wrote, "Oh, if you did know how powerful prayer is for the Salvation of souls! How many interior persons who . . . individually, by prayer alone, have snatched thousands of souls from infidelity, heresy or sin, and raised them to bliss everlasting! Understand, then . . . what you may effect by prayer. . . . If you send only one soul to heaven, you give Me more glory than all men together, on earth, have ever given Me, or can procure for Me. For, whatever glory mortals, on earth, give Me, is limited by the number of acts which are at last finished: but the glory which a blessed soul, in heaven, gives Me – since it is ever-enduring – is equivalent to a number of acts to which there shall be no end forever."

THE GREAT THOUGHT

All of Jesus's teachings are about reaching the place where Jesus is going – Heaven! The entire doctrine of the faith is about the ways and means of reaching eternal life, and all of our work and suffering in this life is but a preparation for a holy death. Our entire focus should be on eternal life.

In the summer, 2002, issue of *From the Housetops*, this powerful meditation on Eternity was given special attention:

"O Mortal, who hast an immortal soul, study, meditate upon, thoroughly realize that great word: ETERNITY.

"I may reckon upon a thousand years, ten thousand years, a hundred million times a thousand years, so many millions of times a thousand years as there are leaves on the trees of the forest, blades of grass on the fields, grains of sand on the sea shore, drops of water in the ocean, stars in the sky; and I have not yet begun to tell what thou art, O ETERNITY!

"And a day will come when the sun shall have ceased to give light, the world shall have been burnt up, the race of man shall have come to an end, the living and the dead shall have been judged, ages upon ages shall be over; and after this, there shall have been abysses of duration since that day of life which passed so quickly; life will appear no longer, save in the immense distance, like those stars which we can scarce perceive, like a dream that has passed away. And there shall be still as much as ever ETERNITY for an ETERNITY!

"For it will always last, it will never end. O always! O never! O ETERNITY! If there is an ETERNITY for me in Heaven, what an inconceivable blessing! Always truth and virtue, life and bliss, the blessed and the Angels.

Always God to contemplate, to love, to possess, to bless, always. And never more any tears, or death, or sorrow, or mourning, never (Apoc 21:4).

"But if there were an ETERNITY reserved for me in Hell, what a terrible misery! Always the stain of sin, always the outer darkness, always the gnawing of worms, always the torment of fire, always imprisonment in chains, always the overflowing of tears, always the gnashing of teeth, always the blasphemies of the damned, always the torments inflicted by devils, always the overwhelming curse of God.

"Always? Always! And never a ray of light to give joy, a moment of sleep to restore, a drop of water to refresh, a friendly word to console. Never to see God, never! O always! O never! O ETERNITY!

"O mortal who has an immortal soul, there is an ETERNITY, and thou hast not a thought of it! Thou hast no thought of it and that ETERNTIY is for thee. And thou art on the brink of that ETERNTIY! And after a few days there will be no more of all those pleasures that amuse thee, of all that business which occupies thee, of all that life which thou abusest.

"ETERNTIY, and thy works, and their fruits. The pleasures of the sinner shall have passed away. But his suffering will remain. And the suffering of the just will have passed away. But his pleasures will remain. Therefore, either the pleasures of time with the sufferings of eternity, or, the sufferings of time with the pleasures of eternity.

"Choose. O ETERNITY! O ETERNITY! I have chosen. I wish to live in Heaven, I wish to live with God. Eternal God, O my sovereign Judge, seized with terror, I throw myself at Your feet. In presence of Your eternity I have no hope save in the greatness of Your mercy and in the bitterness of my repentance. Pardon, pardon me for having run the risk, by my sins, of losing You for ETERNITY. I believe in You and in ETERNITY. I hope in You, and from Your goodness I hope for a happy ETERNTIY. I love You and wish to love You throughout ETERNITY. Strike, use the knife and caustic to my wounds. Spare me not in time but save me, O save me for ETERNITY!"

APPENDIX

OUR LADY OF THE BLESSED SACRAMENT

"O Virgin Mary, Our Lady of the Blessed Sacrament, Thou glory of the Christian people, joy of the Universal Church, salvation of the whole world, pray for us, and awaken in all believers a lively devotion towards the most Holy Eucharist, that so they may be made worthy to partake of the same daily" (Raccolta 418).

SAINT PETER JULIAN EYMARD
Founder of the Blessed Sacrament Fathers, Brothers and Sisters
(France: 1811-1869)

Before whom am I? You are, Holy Church answers me, in the presence of Jesus Christ, your King, your Savior, and your God.

Adore Him, O my soul, with the faith of the man born blind, when on recognizing his benefactor he prostrated himself before Jesus and adored Him most humbly.

Adore Him with the faith of Saint Thomas and say like him: "My Lord and my God" [John 20:28].

But I do not see Jesus like the disciple in the Cenacle; that is true, but our Savior says that they are happier who believe without having seen with their eyes or touched with their hands!

The Church shows me my Savior and my God veiled under the form of a host – as the Precursor showed Him under the form of a simple man, lost in the midst of the crowd, as Mary showed Him to the Magi under the form of a little child.

Adore Him therefore, O my soul, with the faith of the kings of Bethlehem. Offer Him the incense of your adoration, as to your God; the myrrh of your mortification, as to your Savior; the gold of your love and the tribute of dependence, as to your King!

BLESSED ANGELA OF FOLIGNO
Third Order Franciscan (Italy: c. 1248-1309)

O Jesus, You instituted this Sacrament, not through any desire to draw some advantage from it for Yourself, but solely moved by a love which has no other measure than to be without measure. You instituted this Sacrament because Your love exceeds all words. Burning with love for us, You desired to give Yourself to us and took up Your dwelling in the consecrated Host, entirely and forever, until the end of time. And You did this, not only to give us a memorial of Your death which is our salvation, but You did it also, to remain with us entirely and forever.

SAINT KATHARINE DREXEL

Foundress of the Sisters of the Blessed Sacrament (United States: 1858-1955)

I adore You, my Eucharistic God. You are there exposed in the ostensorium [monstrance]. The rays are the rays of Your love for me, for each individual soul. If it wasn't for Your love, I would be in hell. I return You thanksgiving through Mary, through St. Joseph, through all the Apostles, Martyrs, Virgins and Sisters of the Blessed Sacrament in heaven. And lastly, I thank You through the sacred host on all the altars throughout the world.

I adore the host which Jesus instituted to be forever the memorial of His death. I adore my Savior who was crucified, dying and entombed on Calvary . . . . I want now to be present in spirit at the bloody death and suffering endured over 1900 years ago . . . .

O Jesus, I adore You in the host of exposition. This act of adoration by union with it is no trivial act, but will with certitude sanctify and transform my soul. I adore Your heart which desires me to unite myself to your sufferings.

I thank You in union with the angels and with Mary Immaculate for I am a sinner and not worthy to thank You but I know Your Heart will make thanksgiving for me and will make Your Passion bear infinite fruit both in heaven and on earth, so that the citizens of heaven will receive from them an increase of grace, sinners pardon, and the souls in purgatory alleviation of their sufferings.

The sacred host exposed on the altar gives my soul food for "admiration." I admire my Divine Spouse in His humility but above all His love which has placed Him to be there at the words of the priest at consecration. I admire the love which puts Him at the word of every priest in every century . . . . I know that I am a sinner and a big sinner. I have crucified You many times. I praise You for a love beyond my comprehension and yet You have given me the gift of infinite love. I glorify You in union with Mary and beg You to make me imitate this love of Yours . . . . Give me the grace to follow Your will in every detail . . . . I must be all His as He is mine.

SAINT ELIZABETH ANN SETON

Foundress of the Sisters of Charity (United States: 1774-1821)

The words of our Lord are clear enough when taking bread He blessed it, broke it, and gave it to His disciples and said: "Take and eat: this is my Body . . . " I defy Protestants to produce the authority of any of the Fathers of the first four centuries (whom they often quote as good authorities to prove religious truth) in support of their opinion that the words of Jesus Christ in the institution of this sacrament are to be taken in a figurative sense.

154

SAINT BERNARD OF CLAIRVAUX
Cistercian Monk (France: 1090-1153)
Jesus! How sweet is the very thought of You, giving true joy to the heart; but surpassing honey and all sweetness in His own presence. Nothing more sweet can be proclaimed, nothing more pleasant can be heard, nothing more loving can be thought of than Jesus, the Son of God. O Jesus, the hope of penitents, how kind You are to those who pray. How good to those who seek You – but what to those who find! No tongue can tell, nor can the written word express it: only one who knows from experience can say what it means to love Jesus. May You, O Jesus, be our joy as You will be our reward. In You be our glory forever.

BLESSED JOHN XXIII
Pope (Italy: 1881-1963)
We must never forget the visits to the Blessed Sacrament. Modern forms of piety, even when most devout, seem to have less time to spare for this act of homage to Jesus, this keeping him company for a while. Even pious souls are sometimes heard to say: "We live so intensely that we have no time to linger talking with the Lord."

How our soul rejoices when we return to the fervent invocations of St. Alphonsus Liguori, uttered on his visits to the Blessed Sacrament! The horizons seem to lift around us. About these conversations between God and the soul there exists a whole literature, abundant, modern, attractive and enjoyable. Let us turn to it for our consolation, for the hidden delight of days that sometimes seem lukewarm in fervour and full of uncertainties.

VENERABLE PAULINE JARICOT
Foundress of the Society for the Propagation of the Faith (France: 1799-1862)
It is before your holy tabernacles that my heart dried up by cruel trials has constantly found the necessary strength to bear them; there my struggles have become victories, my weakness courage, my lukewarmness fervor, my perplexities have been changed into light, my sadness into joy, obstacles into success, my desires into the will to accomplish them, my antipathies, jealousies, resentments into burning charity. All I have learned at your feet, O Lord; receive therefore the homage of all I am and all that I have, of all I can ever think, say or do that is good.

ARCHBISHOP FULTON J. SHEEN
Writer, Homilist (United States:1895-1979)
God gave us two weapons: knees and hands. Knees—to spend an hour a day in reparation for sins. We begin a national plea for one hour a day of continuous prayer before the Blessed Sacrament . . . . How many of you will answer?

THE SUMMARY OF TRUE CATHOLICISM
The Athanasian Creed

Along with the Apostle's Creed and the Nicene Creed, this is one of the three greatest professions of Faith the Catholic Church uses in her liturgy. For 1500 years Catholic priests have been reciting this Creed.

Whosoever will be saved, before all things it is necessary that he hold the Catholic Faith.

Which Faith except everyone do keep whole and undefiled, without doubt he shall perish everlastingly.

And the Catholic Faith is this: That we worship one God in Trinity, and Trinity in Unity;

Neither confounding the Persons, nor dividing the substance.

For there is one Person of the Father, another of the Son, and another of the Holy Ghost.

The Father uncreate, the Son uncreate, and the Holy Ghost uncreate.

The Father incomprehensible, the Son incomprehensible, and the Holy Ghost incomprehensible.

The Father eternal, the Son eternal, and the Holy Ghost eternal.

And yet there are not three eternals, but one eternal.

As also there are not three incomprehensibles, nor three uncreates, but one uncreate, and one incomprehensible.

So likewise the Father is almighty, the Son almighty, and the Holy Ghost almighty.

And yet they are not three almighties, but one almighty.

So the Father is God, the Son is God, and the Holy Ghost is God.

And yet they are not three Gods, but one God.

So likewise the Father is Lord, the Son is Lord, and the Holy Ghost is Lord.

And yet not three Lords, but one Lord.

For like as we are compelled by the Christian truth to acknowledge every Person by Himself to be God and Lord;

So we are forbidden by the Catholic Religion to say, There be three Gods, or three Lords.

The Father is made of none; neither created, nor begotten. The Son is of the Father alone; not made, nor created, but begotten.

The Holy Ghost is of the Father and of the Son; neither made, nor created, nor begotten, but proceeding.

156

So there is one Father, not three Fathers; one Son, not three Sons; one Holy Ghost, not three Holy Ghosts.

And in this Trinity none is before, or after other; none is greater, or less than another;

But the whole three Persons are co-eternal together, and co-equal.

So that in all things, as is aforesaid, the Unity in Trinity, and the Trinity in Unity is to be worshipped.

He therefore that will be saved must thus think of the Trinity.

Furthermore, it is necessary to everlasting salvation that he also believe rightly the Incarnation of Our Lord Jesus Christ.

For the right faith is, that we believe and confess that Our Lord Jesus Christ, the Son of God, is God and Man;

God, of the substance of the Father, begotten before the worlds; and man, of the substance of His Mother, born in the world;

Perfect God, and Perfect Man, of a reasonable soul and human flesh subsisting;

Equal to the Father, as touching His Godhead; and inferior to the Father, as touching His manhood.

Who although He be God and Man, yet He is not two, but one Christ;

One; not by conversion of the Godhead into flesh, but by taking Manhood into God;

One altogether; not by confusion of substance, but by unity of person.

For as the reasonable soul and flesh is one man, so God and Man is one Christ;

Who suffered for our salvation, descended into Hell, rose again the third day from the dead.

He ascended into Heaven, He sitteth on the hand of the Father, God almighty; from whence He shall come to judge the living and the dead.

At Whose coming all men shall rise again with their bodies, and shall give account for their own works.

And they that have done good shall go into life everlasting; and they that have done evil into everlasting fire.

This is the Catholic Faith, which except a man believes faithfully, he cannot be saved.

Glory be to the Father, and to the Son, and to the Holy Ghost.

As it was in the beginning, is now and ever shall be, world without end. Amen.

"OUTSIDE THE CHURCH THERE IS NO SALVATION"

"Basing itself on Scripture and Tradition, the Council teaches that the Church, a pilgrim now on earth, is necessary for salvation: the one Christ is the mediator and the way of salvation; He is present to us in His body which is the Church. He Himself explicitly asserted the necessity of faith and Baptism, and thereby affirmed at the same time the necessity of the Church which men enter through Baptism as through a door. Hence they could not be saved who, knowing that the Catholic Church was founded as necessary by God through Christ, would refuse either to enter it or to remain in it" (Vatican Council II, Consitution *Lumen Gentium*, No. 14.).

"Those who, through no fault of their own, do not know the Gospel of Christ or His Church, but who nevertheless seek God with a sincere heart, and, moved by grace, try in their actions to do His will as they know it through the dictates of their conscience – those too may achieve eternal salvation" (Ibid., Constitution *Lumen Gentium*, No. 16).

"Although in ways known to Himself God can lead those who, through no fault of their own, are ignorant of the Gospel, to that faith without which it is impossible to please Him (Heb 11:6), the Church still has the obligation and also the sacred right to evangelize all men" (Ibid., Declaration *Ad Gentes*, No. 7).

A PRAYER FOR UNITY
Cardinal Newman

O Lord Jesus Christ, who when Thou wast about to suffer didst pray for thy disciples to the end of time that they might all be one, as Thou art in the Father and the Father in Thee, look down in pity on the manifold division among those who profess Thy faith and heal the many wounds which the pride of man and the craft of Satan have inflicted on Thy people.

Break down the walls of separation which divide one party and denomination of Christians from another. Look with compassion on the souls who have been born in one or other of these communions, which not Thou, but man, has made.

Set free the prisoners from these unauthorized forms of worship and bring them all to the one communion which Thou didst set up at the beginning—the one Holy Catholic and Apostolic Church.

Teach all men that the See of Peter, the Holy Church of Rome, is the foundation, center, and instrument of unity. Open their hearts to the long-forgotten truth that the Holy Father, the Pope, is Thy Vicar and Representative; and that in obeying him in matters of religion, they are obeying Thee, so that as there is but one company in Heaven above, so likewise there may be one communion, confessing and glorifying Thy Holy Name here below.